Born and bred in Lancashire, Ethel Taylor qualified as a doctor, in 1963. She moved to London, slowly climbing the ladder to become a consultant in Geriatric Medicine. Divorced, she has two children and several grandchildren. She divides her time between Israel and London.

Thanks to:

Nick Barlay

Dany Carcea

Writers Group at Tally Ho Corner

To all in the same boat

Ethel Taylor

Woman of her Time

Austin Macauley Publishers™
London • Cambridge • New York • Sharjah

A CIP catalogue record for this title is available from the British Library.

ISBN 9781398482661 (Paperback)
ISBN 9781398482678 (ePub e-book)

www.austinmacauley.com

First Published 2024
Austin Macauley Publishers Ltd®
1 Canada Square
Canary Wharf
London
E14 5AA

Table of Contents

Chapter 1
Life Journal

She was a war baby, born a month after the outbreak of the Second World War. To this day, she only has three inches of water in her bath—at the time, they said even the king and queen used just four. This may have contributed to her puritanical leanings.

The Germans were targeting the nearby AV Roe factory that built the Lancaster Bomber, making her cot bounce up to the ceiling of the shelter as the bombs fell. Undeterred, her father would go out visiting his patients in the corporation houses of Blackley, North Manchester. When she was eighteen months old, he volunteered and left to join the Royal Army medical corps as a captain attached to the Royal Scots Fusiliers in Burma. She didn't see him again until she was five.

By the time he returned, she and her mother had been evacuated, with her grandparents, to a house in Southport as her grandmother had grown panicky at the nightly bombings in Salford.

Life was quiet except for the occasional practice sirens going off. She shared the bedroom with her mother, who had a big jar of Marie biscuits, next to the bed, for munching at night; this wrought havoc with teeth, all filled by ten years old. Her children have no fillings thanks to fluoride tablets, and no food after nightly brushing.

Her first memory is playing with the doll's pram, which her grandfather had bought her, in the lovely garden. She had an imaginary friend, Tom, and a tabby cat, Topsy, whom she stalked, watching her urinate behind the bushes and cover it up with her paws. This excited her but she didn't know why. She made friends with Betty over the garden wall, but her mother stopped the friendship. On her fourth birthday, she waited all afternoon for the guests to arrive at the party and watched her mum whip homemade ice cream. She looked in the dark hall towards the front door, but no one came. The mother had not invited anyone. An Israeli film, *The Summer of Avia*, which she saw much later, had a similar desolate theme, based on a kibbutz just after the war.

The mother was narcissistic; her own mother had a stepmother from a very young age, who never gave her affection and so it got handed down. As a self-interested artist, she painted wonderful flower pictures but couldn't resist gazing into a mirror. Even in her nineties, in a lift, she would turn to look longingly at her reflection.

Standing with her mother at the station, waiting for his train, Ethel was frightened of this strange man in the big Burma hat who strode down the platform towards them. He looked down, smiling delightedly. "Go back to Burma!" she said. She later learned, with pride, that he had fought with Wingate and the Chindits and was awarded the Burma Star, which she still has.

Relegated to the spare room by her grandmother, she missed the mornings in bed next to her mother, who read the blue flimsy airmail letters from far away to her young daughter.

06 01 42

I am at present in Basra, Iraq, awaiting posting. It is bitterly cold here and they are living under canvas. Some of the officers have their meals in their greatcoats. I believe that in a few months, this will be the hottest climate in the world. Everything is frightfully expensive here and the country is very uninteresting and underdeveloped. Gosh, I grumbled about Egypt, but it was wonderful compared to this place. Palestine, of course, was paradise.

Legend has it that the Garden of Eden is near here, but I can't imagine Adam picking a place like this for his Garden of Eden. In any case, I don't blame Eve now for wanting to do things, know things and go places.

Actually, I don't mind all this moving about. It is the gypsy blood in me. It is fun and exciting. It was only a few days ago that I was sunbathing practically in the nude, and now I am shivering with the cold.

I believe the baby is coming along nicely and has quite a lot to say for herself. She says that her daddy is in "opistal in the Middle East." How I would love to see her now. But I will have to wait until this wretched war is over.

08 08 43

Well, I am on my war leave and spending it in Madras. It is very hot but a nice change from the monsoon and after living under canvas and mud up to your knees. I am staying in a nice hotel here. I have left the hospital and am a regimental medical officer with an infantry regiment. My present job is certainly more dangerous than being in a base hospital and I may come up against some tight corners. As for myself, I am quite happy and prepared to accompany the officers in their campaign. "Please don't say much to Mother."

That closeness with her mother was gone but a new one grew, as she began to love her father; coming to know him as a quiet, solid, kind man who could be fun. His made-up stories of Lettuce Watercress, the antics of a nursemaid, at bedtime, were told to her own children. "Called to look after the princesses in Buckingham Palace, she lost one in the park."

They moved back to Manchester, and her father resumed his general practice in Blackley. She loved his dispensary, a narrow galley, the anteroom to the surgery and the waiting room beyond. She would help to label the brightly coloured bottles of medicine for cough or dyspepsia, wrapping them in crisp white paper. Going out on visits with him, discussing diagnoses—her wish to become a doctor all stemmed from these early days.

He took her on long walks down country lanes in Bamford, or Simister Lane. The fresh air, greenery, and farmyard smells—a magical escape from the grim corporation housing estate. After he was gone, she'd wander off exploring the surrounding fields for hours, happy on her own, and continued this routine during the many difficult years that followed. It was safe then. Summer holidays were spent with grandparents in Southport, reached on the train from Victoria station. Her mother would leave her in the care of a "nice lady," and Grandma would pick her up at Chapel Street.

She loved swinging in the hammock and reading in the sunshine in the beautiful garden. She'd pick a crispy green Miller apple, milky white inside, from the trees, planted by her grandfather, and in the evening she would follow him around the warm, heavily fragrant greenhouse as he watered the tomatoes, cucumbers, and vine. She learnt how to tend to these plants; today, the smell of vine tomatoes takes her back to those times. Her grandma would take her to Bournemouth, Torquay, and Blackpool to kosher hotels, leaving Grandpa at home. She enjoyed the trips, but felt envious of the loud, happy families, holidaying together, when her parents preferred vacationing without her.

She only had her daddy to herself for five years, as terrible screams emanating from her parents' bedroom at night plus hearing her mother run downstairs to ring her parents, were the herald of the coming breakup. Her father had naively confessed his peccadilloes with beautiful Indian women, on his first night home, and her mother couldn't swallow it. She had waited faithfully five years for his return under the strict eye of her grandfather.

Her mother was the original drama queen. Ethel remembers biting the thermometer once, and as the mercury ran out in little silver balls, she shouted, "You're going to die, you're going to die!" and then forced cotton wool sandwiches down her throat.

In 1948, a double milestone in their house occurred with the advent of the National Health Service. Bevan, the goodie, and much talk around the table. No more dispensing at home, no more her father letting the poor off their bills. Instead, being called out to a house to move the wardrobe—"Let the doctor do it, it's free." Bevan promising to stuff the doctors' mouths with gold; some of the medical professionals felt they had been sold down the river.

Then came the excitement of the establishment of the State of Israel. Sitting around the wireless listening to the United Nations vote—Micronesia, yes, Russia, yes, UK, abstained. Bevin, the baddie, sent the ships, full of Holocaust survivors, back from the shores of Palestine to Germany and Cyprus. On the day after the British left their mandate of Palestine, the Arabs attacked and the agony of the War of Independence with its siege of Jerusalem began.

Sitting on the stairs, eavesdropping, she realised her mum was developing a romance with the assistant, a refugee whom her father had taken into his home and given a job. Demobbed from General Ander's British Army, he was one of the many Poles attracted to the Polish Jewish community in Manchester. He was the second tall, blond veteran to lodge in our house, the first having been thrown out by her father, rightly suspicious of chatting up her mother. A pity 'cause she liked that one.

One morning, while waiting for the car to heat up, choke out, to take her to school in Alkrington, her father told her he had made Dr P a partner in the practice. Sadly, she said, "He'll never leave this house now, Daddy." She was so right and she had hated him at first sight, saying "You stink" when he came for an interview. She probably wasn't nice but children know.

So, it was her father who left the house. Ostensibly to spend a year in Jerusalem, doing his beloved dermatology in Hadassah hospital and to live with his mother, who had gone there to die in the Holy Land. Another railway station memory, after a cinema visit to see Easter Parade. They saw her father off, a strange and dark moment. It was very British:

no explanation, just goodbye, then a quiet drive back to the house.

Now her troubles began in earnest, she started Manchester High School for Girls on a foundation scholarship, travelling on two buses in and out of town to get there. She made a friend named Margaret.

"I took a packed lunch of a dried-up cheese sandwich to school and came home to make myself another cold sandwich or fry an egg for supper. So I suggested to my mother that she leave a potted version of the main meal they had eaten at lunch time. I was happy to find a small blue Creuset pot of stew or a miniature version of their spaghetti Bolognese waiting for me to heat up after my long journey home. She just had not realised the omission, so immersed in her own bubble. It wasn't actual neglect."

One day, she came home from school to find her favourite uncle, Robert, and her Aunt Serena having tea, the table festively set. She always loved it when he was around, so interesting, benign, and gentle. She remembered him, as a measly four-year-old, in a darkened room, sitting on the edge of her bed in his captain's uniform, as he proved Pythagoras's theorem simply with a diagram. What a compliment to a little girl.

She settled down to enjoy the unexpected food and company. When she had finished, he asked her to accompany him for a walk; she agreed, totally unaware of the news she was about to hear. He turned to her and said, "Your mother asked me to come and tell you that today, your parents got divorced. The court case was this afternoon and she wanted you to know before other people might tell you." Shocked, she went on walking, passing by a neighbour and smiling and greeting, saying, "Hello." Her uncle commented, "That's very brave of you to do that."

In a quiet, conversational tone, he continued, "One of the reasons for the divorce was that your mother couldn't cope with your father's confession on his first night back from five years away fighting." She knew there was a more pressing reason sitting at their very dining room table but she said nothing. The visitors departed. Nobody said anything. She went to bed.

The next day at school, Margaret announced that her brother-in-law, a lawyer, had been there at the court proceedings so she knew everything. She commented, "My parents said it would have been better if your father had died. Now, whenever you walk into a room, people will talk about it." Such was the stigma of divorce in the early '50s. How it was to change, now touching 40 per cent of marriages. Even in the royal family, three out of four of the queen's children are divorced.

Chapter 2
Survival

She was now faced with a strange situation, eleven years old and entering puberty. There were two Polish doctors living in the house, sharing a bedroom. One, the Dr P aforementioned. The second, brought in to act as an assistant in the practice when her father left. Dr Stein was a kindly bachelor who advanced her literary education, getting her to read Thomas Mann's Magic Mountain, Andre Gide, Malraux, and Proust, books she would never have come across otherwise. He wore a hair net over his perfumed, oiled head at night and had walked over the Pyrenees with a broken leg to escape the Germans.

Dr Stein was the one who told her that salad without a dressing of oil and vinegar was somehow wrong, tasteless in keeping with English food. That was the '50s. Now, they wouldn't think of serving such a naked salad. She never asked what was for tea; it was nearly always boiled eggs. Pasta, pizza, and yoghurt came much later with the Common Market.

On her twelfth birthday, she came home from school to find he had bought her a cocker spaniel, named Brandy. Her mother, deciding that she was too excited, banished her to the kitchen to learn the Psalm, a fine for talking during Jewish prayers.

Mother came to despise poor Dr Stein, throwing him hateful glances at the dinner table and complaining about him constantly. She had a habit of these sudden dislikes. He left to marry a young patient.

The house was big and gabled, surrounded by Rhododendron shrubberies in which she used to play. It was a purpose-built doctor's house with its own entrance to the waiting room and surgery and situated in a corporation estate. At the back was a washhouse holding a mangle and washtub. As she studied in her bedroom, she'd hear the blackbirds singing in the garden in the spring. When the noisy, black-faced coal men came to pour their sacks of coal down the chute, her mother would count the bags.

Her bedroom was really a dressing room off the main bedroom with an adjoining door. Hearing Dr P leave his bedroom at night, followed by the squeaking of her mother's bed, was shocking, her imagination overworking. She tried to block it out, by burrowing under the bedclothes. Once she even called out, "I can hear you."

An unpleasant start to her adolescence. Eventually, they moved to the refurbished junk room across the hall.

When she visited her grandparents in Southport (she was often bundled off), she told them, crying, that she had heard him in her mother's bedroom at night. They were emphatic that Dr P had married her mother secretly and not told her, on her Uncle Robert's advice. "She doesn't like him. Let her get used to him first." Finding the passport in a drawer with her mother's new married name was a bitter confirmation of the fact. A big mistake, which resulted in wagging tongues in the Jewish community, never mind the local council estate.

Dr P enjoyed teasing and mocking her. An example was, him saying, sneering, "I saw you crossing the road in town today with your hockey stick," copying the way she walked. Her mother would say, "It's good for you, darling, as you never had a brother to tease you."

Psychosomatic tummy pains developed in response to the nadir of her young life. It is now known that it takes a strong character to sublimate their problems into physical symptoms.

Next on the agenda, her stepfather stopped her mother and her from having their own separate GP, saying that he was the best person to treat them. If not illegal, it was and is a strongly discouraged practice in England. His Machiavellian motive subsequently became clear.

In the disingenuous guise of her family GP, he offered to examine her to see whether her abdominal pains were due to her oncoming menarche.

Without a chaperone, she lay there unsuspecting in her childish bedroom, while he proceeded to inspect her down below. Hearing heavy breathing, she looked up to see his red face leering and a sudden realisation swept over her. She jumped up, pushing him away, and he left. She never again saw such a picture of perverted lust.

She realised what she was dealing with, but in those days, it was a taboo subject both within the family as well as society at large. That taboo coerces you and everyone into silence and leads to real difficulty in getting past it. She told her mother, of course. Helpless, one awful day, she watched her sobbing daughter pull her scorched little diary from the open fire, into which he had thrown it, after reading her account of his behaviour. Mother appeared to believe his denials; now it's called collusion.

Much later, Mrs P revealed that when she consulted grandfather, he advised, "Do nothing! You have already been divorced once." From then on, if he passed her in the corridor, Dr P would grab her from the front, hovering outside the bathroom door whenever she had a bath, chasing her around the dinner table. He even fished her knickers out of the washing basket and came downstairs, smelling them appreciatively, grinning. "What a lovely smell."

Only once did Rex hit her, her nose bleeding onto Brandy's head as she wept and held her spaniel for some emotional succour. She thinks this incident brought her father to return from Israel. When he received her explicit letter, he went to the professor and said, "I must go back to England. My daughter needs me."

She never could relax in her own home.

Ethel never succumbed and many years later, a clever cousin, who wheedled the story out of her for the first time at the age of thirty, explained that the cause of his cruelty to her was revenge for her refusals. Her stepfather called her "L'addition," which she always thought meant "the extra" to her mother, but as her French improved, she realised it was "the price," the bill for taking on her mother.

Chapter 3
Happy Holidays

There were some good times that could be called "Escape from Colditz" or "hobnobbing with the enemy." At sixteen, she was invited to join her parents, mainly to prevent her from mixing with the opposite sex at youth group camps.

Lovely holidays, driving through France to Italy or Spain. Rex (his name now) seemed to have friends everywhere. He had fought in the Battle of Monte Cassino and thus spoke fluent Italian, learnt as pillow talk, from a blonde countess, Ada. He liked flaunting photos of them together in Pesaro, where she lived.

They used to motor through the French countryside, stopping for a lunch of bread, cheese, and delicious patisserie such as apple chausson, then drive on to the next destination and look for a place to stay. In the evening, they would walk around, sometimes drag, getting tired, as he compared the prices of every restaurant in town for dinner. Rex was frugal. The South of France was idyllic then. The sumptuous gardens surrounding the villas, viewed from the Grande Corniche with glimpses of the deep blue Mediterranean, are still vivid in her memory.

Once, they stopped off in Menton for a few days, eating ratatouille for the first time in the sunny garden of the hotel. They always ended the meal with wonderful soft cheeses and fruit. She cut a large peach in two, releasing an earwig which ran across the table as they all screamed. She is still nervous about opening a peach, afraid of what's going to jump out. Could be a metaphor for life.

She remembers discussing a blind little girl who was there; it had just been discovered that the high oxygen in her premature baby's incubator had caused retrolental fibroplasia. Since then, the oxygen concentration is kept below 40 per cent. Disappointed to return recently to the area to find it a little jaded, but maybe it was just her mood.

Arriving in Rome, they looked up Leo de Capua, a violinist in the opera, and were invited for Spaghetti Napolitana by his wife in their small sitting room. He gave them tickets to spend two magical nights, sitting in the open air at Caracalla, the Roman amphitheatre. Aida was unforgettable, the spectacle of the real elephants, the rich music with familiar choruses, and the Egyptian scenery.

Another trip, driving via Carcassonne, the walled city, and through ravishing Provence to Barcelona. Even there, Rex found an old friend with twin daughters, her age. They went with them to the reopening of the old synagogue. It is always good to visit people in their own home when abroad. It's a lesson in how they live and replaces that estranged feeling with one of familiarity, ersatz as it may be. For her, it was a taste of an ideal home.

They always spent the last week in Paris, Rex's alma mater. They stayed in little pensions around the Rue de L'École de Médecine, walking down his memory lane as he pointed out places he had stayed in as a student. She recalled the inscription on the statue of Claude Bernard, saying he had discovered diabetes by tasting his patients' sweet urine.

In fact, Maimonides (Rambam) was the first to savour urine to diagnose diabetes, eight hundred years before, as physician to the Pasha in Egypt. Rex had a very good Polish friend from his medical student days. He was a plastic surgeon with his own clinic near the Jardin des Plantes. He begged to operate on her broken nose, sustained running around the school playground, but she refused. Vanity was not as important as safety for her. Georges, as they called him, was very good-looking and charming; they all loved him. His dentist wife, Corinne, blonde, chic, with her own salon de beaute for men in Place Vendome, was very avant-garde in those days. Corinne took mother and daughter to a fashion show, which they adored, feeling part of the French sophisticated scene.

Three years later, Corinne appeared unkempt and bedraggled with twisted stockings. They didn't realise but this was the beginning of her tragic decline into schizophrenia. Georges had married her unaware that her father had suffered from this hereditary disease. He was forced to divorce her after she had spent years in an institution and was devastated when his only son developed it as well.

Anyhow, they were glamorous times, as they were taken to famous restaurants such as Closerie des Lilacs, Au Deux Maggots, and Brasserie Lipp, all frequented by the impressionists and existentialists. "Look, I'm sure that's Sartre over there. Is he a friend of yours?" she naively asked, having seen photos of him in Simone de Beauvoir's book. Other happy memories were dancing in the street on quatorze

Juillet with Georges's medic nephew, who was rescued from the camps by Georges after the Holocaust and adopted by him.

Georges bought a chateau which they visited in the country in his Citroen DS19 (dess or goddess), a revolutionary spaceship, famous for its hydro-pneumatic suspension; when the key was put in the ignition, the car rose in the air. She remembered being ill from kosher pickled meat he had found especially for her.

Back home, there was the old relapse into her stepfather's cruelty. He was given the job of handing over her pocket money, arranged by her father through the caretaker at the other surgery. He would throw it at her with a sneer. "This is from your loving daddy," implying its meagreness.

Otherwise, she managed to sublimate her problems into studying. It kept her mind off things, which wasn't difficult as the material was so absorbing. Throughout, she kept mostly to herself, coming home from school, having something to eat alone in the kitchen while her mother read the *Manchester Evening News* in the dining room, and then going to her room to do homework. Listening to *The Goon Show* was a fun break. She would come down for a while to watch TV with her mother and have a snack such as a lettuce sandwich. *That Was the Week That Was*, a jokey review with David Frost. On April Fool's, they were not taken in at the harvesting of spaghetti from the trees in Italy. She always disappeared hastily upstairs when Rex appeared from his late evening surgery, to get away from any further artillery.

Chapter 4
First Love

The summer of 1956 saw her at fifteen encountering the agony and ecstasy of first love.

She had just finished her O-Levels when her father informed her that she had acquired a baby sister from his second marriage to Gloria, an old friend from his student days in Dublin. "Her name is Mia." Hurt to the core, she cried, "That's my middle name."

"Oh," he replied, "I forgot." She felt denigrated to the point of nonexistence by her own father. He had already abandoned her twice to the wolves and this was further evidence of his empty love. Anyhow, as it turned out, Mia is one of the best things that happened to her, one of the gifts her father gave to her along with a love of music and medicine.

As usual, the summer holidays found her staying in Scarisbrick New Road in Southport with her grandparents. Accustomed to going to synagogue in Manchester with her best friend Margaret, most Sabbaths, she set off on the long walk to the Southport shul in Arnside Road. She was wearing a new beige and white suit with a red and white spotted floppy beret. She found some friends in the front row of the ladies' gallery and sat with them.

During the service, Marlene pointed to a tall, young blond boy in the front row; he was looking up at her. "That's Tom. He's brilliant, going to Cambridge." She looked straight into his eyes, and in that moment it felt like a "coup de foudre," their intense gazes locked for a few seconds; she felt excited. The service carried on; she was looking forward to meeting him after several surreptitious looks in his direction. Pumping Marlene, she learned that he had topped all of England in his law exams. He already had a brother, studying medicine at Caius College, Cambridge.

Finally, they went downstairs to the courtyard to join the men who were greeting their womenfolk and chatting. There he was, again, staring at her. Marlene introduced them. She looked up into his hazel eyes and smiled, a lengthening moment of stillness, recognition, some small talk, and then goodbye; she was walking back home alone.

Of course, she told her grandparents at a lunch of crispy roast potatoes and braised chicken that she had met Tom Barrow. Her grandfather, reminiscing at the table, "Barrow owed me money once. After some years he came to pay me back. I told him to give it to charity." That figured, one of her grandpa's axioms which they all hold to this day was, "Never lend money unless you assume you are not going to get it back."

Tom sent her a postcard from Loch Lomond. "The misty mountains at the far end of the lake blend beautifully with the serenity of the still water." Remembered verbatim.

Thus began a deliriously happy time being part of a young group enjoying the long vac before going up to Cambridge. Tom, his brother, Peter, a physics student living around the corner, and a small hyperactive, brilliant medical student,

Bernard, who remained a pal till the end of his life. They would go to a coffee bar, a great new "in" thing then on Lord Street, the beautiful tree-lined shopping street in Southport, or meet in the Barrows' house or garden. She still has the photograph of Tom pointing a garden rake at her. Her father, grinning like a Cheshire cat, called him "the rake" after this.

She moved on from Southport to stay with her father, his new wife, and baby in Bispham Road, Blackpool, a red brick purpose-built doctor's house. Life was a bit crazy there as Gloria's "Viennese Opera" type, henna-haired mother was staying from Dublin together with her two single, ageing bachelor brothers.

Tom et al visited her for the day, which went by in a haze of jollity. In the evening, they congregated in the living room of a friend, Ruth, whose house looked out onto the sea in St Annes. Ethel had the stirring experience of the "black void" for the first time whilst dancing with Tom. They looked into each other's eyes so deeply and so long that something seemed to move in the darkness of his eyes. It has only happened twice more in her life. After the visit, she'd lie in bed in a dream going over that lovely day.

Back in Manchester, coming home from school, her mother had stuck his letter up on the windowpane around the front door addressed to "Ethel" from him, of course full of news of his Cambridge life.

New Year's Eve was coming up and she decided to have a party. Her stepfather was against parties so the planning took place in secret; it was arranged they go to friends on the night to get them out of the way. Her mother, a good hostess, made sangria as a welcome. Bernard appeared early from Liverpool; she had been forewarned to be ready by her mother, who said, “Someone always arrives too early.” It was to be an exciting party. Tall, smiling Tom arrived with Peter behind; the excitement had begun. A reveller removed the front door and Ethel shook, worrying what her stepfather would say.

In the kitchen, she sabotaged her whole life. She was standing by the black Aga with Tom when he gave her a white box holding a bottle of perfume with the word “admiration” written on it in purple-pink. She took it, hardly believing this godly object. Only years of therapy managed to explain why she spoilt this wonderful moment by saying, “Do you want it back?” He shook his head, with a little smile then a friend rushed in and broke the tension. He went out. Crack! Why did she do such a stupid thing? She thinks she lost him at that point. She had felt unworthy of such a gift after years of Rexian putdowns and that is the only explanation. The party ended, they left, and she treasured that box of perfume for years. Tom became elusive. She chased him, bad advice from her mum, who regretted not having chased a cousin she had loved.

He gave her another chance which she once again grievously smashed. One spring evening, months later, she was dissecting worms from the garden as homework for A-Level zoology in her father’s surgery in Blackpool, when the phone rang. It was Tom, asking if he had left a raincoat in their house in Manchester after the party. Then he invited her to the May Ball in Cambridge. A dream destroyed! She priggishly said, “She can’t go, as she is still a schoolgirl. It’s not suitable.” Bitterly regretting this forever especially when her own daughter, years later went with her future husband to a May Ball.

This self-destructive instinct became a recurrent pattern whenever she felt secure in someone's affection.

That summer of 1956 was punctuated by the beginning of the Sinai campaign. The family was glued to the wireless. Nasser nationalised the Suez Canal to pay for the Aswan Dam as America and the World Bank had opted out of their agreement to finance it. This was a disaster for the British Empire to lose its key connection, which Disraeli had bought in 1875 for four million pounds.

A secret agreement was made, near Paris, by the prime ministers of France, England, and Israel, that Israel should attack Egypt as a pretext for an Anglo-French invasion of Suez. Moshe Dayan led the attack, taking the Mitla Pass. Rex's young cousin lost his kidney there in a tank battle.

The Labour Party forced a shameful back-off by Anthony Eden, endorsed by America. Britain, as a force in the Middle East, never mind the world, was finished, mirroring her own loss. Mother cancelled the *Manchester Guardian* after its blatant Labour support, as did most of the Jewish community in Manchester.

Ethel's heart breaks each time she thinks of her fateful rejection of that tentative offering of love, as exquisite as the first spring snowdrops.

Chapter 5
Medical School

Ethel passed her O-Levels and started A-Level zoology, chemistry, and physics, required for the medicine she had set her heart on. On the bus to Manchester High School, she would look longingly at the pseudo-Gothic medical school wondering if she would ever go there. The physics was hard. Such a big jump; she could barely understand the textbook English at first. Her mother paid for her to walk over to Manchester Grammar, after school, for physics coaching, and with hard graft she managed to scrape a pass, keeping in mind Churchill's message that a pass is what matters, not the grade.

Jubilant at her successful A-Level results, she wanted to tell her grandparents in Southport, but her mother wouldn't let her use the telephone for an expensive trunk call during the day. She had to walk to the nearest phone box in Victoria Avenue, fifteen minutes away. This was deflating and mean of her; Ethel suspected it was a little jealousy, as Grandpa would not let her mother go to university. Although supported her every step of the way in her wish to do medicine, by obtaining and paying for private tuition.

Rex brainwashed her endlessly to become a dentist. Weak and easily influenced, she gave in. At the end of her interview for the Manchester dental school, which involved an awful, practical turning a square of some pliable material into a pyramid, she was asked if she had any questions. "Yes, after I've finished dentistry, can I study medicine?" The professor replied, "If I were you, I'd go across the road and apply at the medical school now." She took his advice. When Rex heard this, he said, "I forgot that you have hands of clay and couldn't be a good dentist." He was justifying himself because she was quite dexterous in piano, playing to grade six, even embroidery, stitching beautiful tablecloths. He did overreact whenever she dropped something, yelling, "Shlamile."

Her first year at medical school began. She was so proud of her dark blue and gold striped scarf, remembering the kudos her Cambridge friends had attached to their Gonville and Caius dark and pale blue scarves. She took it to Southport, flaunting it around town, but Grandpa did not seem so impressed, probably thinking she was being childish.

Next, she had to buy her real skeleton, Charlie, the traditional name, who hung in her bedroom for two years keeping her company, as she studied for the three-weekly anatomy vivas.

They had to venture into the dissecting room of dead bodies, a large, airy room lined with stands on which lay the self-donated cadavers. It had a special smell, a combination of formalin and rotting flesh. Only yesterday, she was reminded of it when she opened a bottle of Tabasco.

They worked painstakingly with special scalpels, following arteries, nerves, and muscles and identifying anomalies from our *Cunningham's Manual* and *Gray's Anatomy*. They took it seriously and respectfully, so she was shocked when Rex told her that as students in Paris, they had chopped off a penis and put it into the handbag of a girl they judged as loose. Ethel coped, along with her anatomy partner, Jacky, who used to sing "Kiss Me Honey, Honey Kiss Me" quite cheerfully whilst at work.

The studies were put on hold when her grandfather had a severe stroke; she wanted to go to Southport to be with him, her mother was against this but Rex said, "Let her go."

Brought downstairs in his double bed, he lay there unconscious, breathing heavily. A maiden aunt, a nurse who incidentally had helped to deliver her, had been called to look after him. Grandma hovered at the end of the bed, helpless. The family gathered around. The doctor decided not to treat him with antibiotics for inevitable pneumonia, known as the old man's friend; her Uncle Robert, also a doctor, agreed. At that time, reserpine was the only treatment for his high blood pressure and not very effective, causing depression as a side effect.

They were asleep at the end and when they awoke, he had gone. She saw him looking peaceful and rather beautiful.

He had been a handsome man. At nineteen, he emigrated from Dvinsk in White Russia to work as a miner in Wales. One day, he heard the others say, "Push the truck in front of that bloody Jew!" He left, travelled to Manchester, learnt tailoring, and opened a raincoat factory with a partner, Mr Holbein. The raincoats were marketed as Holbort. She used to go to the factory in Moulton Street, up the steep stairs, to fit one for school.

The grandfather became a pillar of the community, founding synagogues, Bne Brit lodges, and the cemetery he was buried in. He was a self-made man par excellence. One of the first to have a car with a chauffeur because he was blind in one eye from trachoma, caught in Russia. Always up to date, the first to read *Dr. Zhivago*. He was a powerful man too; her mother claimed he forced her to marry her father, saying he would throw her out of the house if she refused. Ethel loved him. He was her father figure and walked her to Kew Preparatory nursery school along Scarisbrick New Road.

She remembered Grandma crying, “I’ll never see him again,” as they took him away.

They escorted “him” back to Manchester, where the tradition was that women did not attend the funeral but waited at home. The May blossom was out as she recalled each year on his yahrzeit (the anniversary of his death).

Her mother was only interested in washing her hair and she overheard them talking loudly in the night about the will, as she cried in her bedroom at her mother’s callousness and injustice, at the loss of that strong and benign father figure in her life. She went back over the times in Southport; she had sat on his knee as he dried her long hair or joined him for a second breakfast after he came downstairs late. Walking out with his silver-topped cane after she had fastened spats over his shoes.

Grandma stayed with them for the week of the shiva, the traditional Jewish mourning period. Rex cruelly called her a peacock for her love of colourful clothes and diagnosed her as an alcoholic as she took to brandy to get through her grief. Shiva means seven in Hebrew. The chief mourners eat a meal of hardboiled eggs to represent the full circle of life. Then they have to sit on low stools, wearing slippers or canvas shoes (leather is forbidden as it equals comfort), the men unshaven for the rest of the week, when people visit. It is a very therapeutic thing to be surrounded by close family, greeting friends and relatives. Grandfather had brought his brothers and sisters over from Russia when he could afford it, so there were lots of relatives around. Her stepfather was impressed when police had to direct the traffic, as so many attended his funeral.

Uncle Robert left after a few days, disgusted by the whole affair. He had married a non-Jewish girl who had converted to Judaism to marry but then baptised her only son. Grandpa had received an anonymous letter informing him of this. She had never laughed so much as at a distant relative, who was an expert in telling Yiddish jokes accompanied by actions, such as ironing by a poor tailor; he kept us entertained.

Re-entering the dissecting room was traumatic after her grandfather's death. Seeing the pale dead bodies must have reminded her; she almost fainted and had to take hold of herself.

> I especially loved histology, looking down the microscope or cine projections of the colourful variegated cells characteristic of each organ. The square cyclamen cubes of liver tissue, the flat squashed squamous cells of the skin and learning the normal configurations. Later in pathology, spotting infiltrations of leucocytes and lymphocytes in clumps revealing an infection or even an abscess. Tuberculosis had its own tell-tale giant cells. Purple staining material may signal amyloid (porridge in Greek) of the dread Alzheimer.

During this period, her friend was Marietta, a fellow medical student. Her parents took them to their tiny London flat for those few critical days awaiting their second MB results in anatomy and physiology. The night they heard they had passed was unforgettable: dinner in a Chinese restaurant on Shaftesbury Avenue and then going to the Royal Festival Hall to hear Beethoven's Ninth Symphony. Exhilaration flared with the final chorus of "*An die Freude*," ("Ode to Joy"), merging with the anticipation of starting clinical work on the wards. Real medicine at last! The freedom and academic thrill of actually dealing with diseases, which she had only read about, was intoxicating.

Chapter 6
Starting Clinicals

Medical school was turning out to be just an extension of school; the same bus journeys from north to south Manchester. All-day lectures and practicals. Ethel had wanted to go to London to get away but wasn't allowed. Her stepfather said that home was better to cope with studies; she thought the reason was financial. He was right, though, as the course was intensive—no time for running a flat in a new city. So she decided to join medic Revue to get some taste of varsity life. Twice-weekly rehearsals meant she came home late in the evenings flushed and animated. Mother, sitting at home, reading the paper, became angry each time, saying, "It was all too much for her." Was envy or possessiveness behind this wearing down her enthusiasm? Anyhow, it was a cause of tension and spoiled the fun of being part of the troupe.

The night of the show arrived. She had a part dancing in the chorus of *Dance of the Hours*, dressed in a white tutu, her arms up in the air, lolloping on to the stage. She knew she was a glomp but that was the idea, supposedly funny. Rex had been dragged along in support retaliated by mocking and sneering with a horrible laugh, copying her awful act on the stage for weeks afterwards. Total antagonism to the whole project from square one.

However, nothing stopped her love of being on the wards, her stethoscope around her neck. They gathered around a patient's bed learning to examine always from the left side. On one occasion, Sir Robert Platt, president of the Royal College of Physicians, called her out to palpate a lady's abdomen; he was pleased when she picked out an enlarged kidney. The fine art of auscultation for heart murmurs; using a stethoscope had to be acquired by listening very hard first, to the normal two sounds, "bu boom," then identifying any added sounds like "bu whoosh boom," signifying flow problems in the valve.

Later, they saw various diseases and read them up at night in heavy textbooks. Surgery was not left out. An early attendance in theatre was grim; the professor, an ill man himself with a bamboo spine was so rough, the patient died on the table. Perhaps he had expedited it as she was so terminally ill. Something she never saw again.

Then the fun part—residency at St Mary's in Oxford Road for midwifery. She learnt to play bridge, whilst waiting to be called to the labour ward. It was the first time she had really been away from home for so long: She felt carefree but was unaware of the significance, but now she can see it was freedom from the oppressive atmosphere.

They had to deliver ten babies and stay after the delivery to wash the newborns and all the dirty equipment. It was dawn, and the mother was in a confiding mood, telling her that her husband was not the father of the child. She learnt much later that this is a national statistic; one in ten fathers are still bringing up infants not their own.

The harsh alarm jolted them out of bed in the early hours of one morning, and the group hurried to the hot crowded labour room. There, the mother was panting, her neck veins distended as she pushed hard. Ethel already felt woozy from the low blood sugar and the tense atmosphere, which she was not yet used to. When the baby appeared, she watched horror-struck, feeling faint, as the reddened, wriggling, deformed boy with stumps for arms and legs was born. Confused, they filed out quietly. The mother, an unmarried midwife herself, had taken the anti-nausea tablet in her early pregnancy and produced a thalidomide child. The irony of this disaster was the full-page advert in the medical journals implying how safe it was. It showed a healthy toddler climbing up on tiptoes to open a medicine cabinet and taking out a tablet from the bottle.

After passing the pathology and bacteriology of third M.B., her father offered to take her with him to Israel to put up the memorial stone for his mother, who had gone there ten years previously to die. She had only met this grandmother once when she stayed with them en route from Dublin to Israel. She was a slightly fearsome woman, never smiling and wearing a sheitel, a wig worn by orthodox married women beholden to cover their hair. They gave her scrambled eggs made of the yellow dried powder still only available after the war.

In 1961, the price of the ticket was 120 pounds, comparing amazingly with the price of an Easy Jet ticket of the same amount today, sixty years later. Excited, as it was the first time she had flown, she looked down at the snowy Alps and then traced the Greek coastline, orange against the blue sea. They landed at tiny Lod airport, virtually a shack; the country was only thirteen years old then, so everything was a bit primitive. Her father spoke fluent Hebrew and they got themselves to her grandmother's empty basic flat in Bayit Vegan, a suburb of Jerusalem, in the dark by taxi. The next morning, she walked to the tiny makolet, a grocer's shop with everything bursting at the seams, and bought fresh buns and cartons of leben, sour curds and whey, a delicious food. Walking through the mountain pines with their special fragrance to get the single-decker No. 12 bus, they made their way to the mason to choose the marble wording for the gravestone.

Her father had friends from the time he worked in Hadassah hospital, so they were very busy. One friend, a professor of bacteriology, called her a "chaticha," a big compliment in his eyes. It meant "piece" in Hebrew but was slang for a beautiful bacteria or pretty girl. Flattered, she used it as her first password when email came along. They did visit the Mandelbaum Gate, the checkpoint separating Jerusalem from the Jordanian part at the ceasefire line. High walls had to be built to protect passersby from sniper shots. Ethel and her father wandered through Mea Shearim, the extreme orthodox area, where black-hatted, white-stockinged men strolled, then had lunch of gefilte fish in a Shtisel-type basic café.

He had arranged for her to join a four-week tour of Israel with Habonim, a pioneer scout movement. He dropped her off at Kibbutz Tsora, Samson's birthplace out in the Jerusalem hills, and went home. This trip was an excellent introduction to her lifelong association and love of the Holy Land. Being with British young people, staying in kibbutzim, they toured this small country extensively with guides. They explained the archaeological sites, some of them living proof of the historical accuracy of the Bible. Avdat in the Negev was a good example. They dug exactly where the scripture described, so many hectares north and east of Beersheva, and found this ancient city. They stayed in Eilat in a youth hostel, the town almost empty then, with only one small nightclub on the beach called Sof Haolam (End of the World). Now it's an international resort with glitzy palatial hotels.

Singing and dancing folk dances, they spent ten days picking figs on kibbutz Bet Haemek in the Galil, rising at 5 a.m. when it was cooler. Mike Leigh, the renowned director, was in their group and directed their show at the end. He was a round-faced, enthusiastic lad from Manchester, a vague relative. Twenty versions of "Waiter, waiter, I've got a fly in my soup" were presented. The kibbutz youth woke them one morning after switching on and redirecting the rotating sprinklers to their tents, drenching them.

She returned refreshed to take on the gynaecology course. All medical students think they have some terrible disease, so when she developed intermenstrual bleeding, she decided she had a growth after looking at the books. She told her father who was working in Lytham. He arranged for her to see a gynaecologist. She needed an EUA, an examination under anaesthesia, usual for virgo intacta. After much personal agonising, she went to Lytham. There was snow on the ground; she took herself to the cottage hospital. No one visited her. After the operation, she crept into the sister's office and read the notes. She had had a cervical polyp removed—vindicated!

When she got back to Manchester, all hell was let loose when she told Rex why she had been to Lytham. Her stepfather in a shouting purple rage, "You will never get married—you have lost your virginity!" To her incredulity and shame, he rang up the surgeon in Lytham demanding that he stitch up her hymen. The poor doctor, an English gentleman, explained that this was not done, and it would probably heal anyway. The story reached a fellow local medical student. She was hot inside with dread as he smiled knowingly and mentioned he knew her father in Lytham. Maybe it was paranoia, but embarrassing nevertheless. It did not get out, to her relief, so he kept his counsel.

Another paddy occurred when Rex heard that she had passed her driving test the first time, having sold her skeleton to pay for driving lessons. He stormed out of the kitchen saying, "You have no right to have passed." Her mother and she laughed but he didn't speak to her for weeks. They were used to his temper tantrums.

Chapter 7
A Hungarian Beau

Residency for paediatrics was a happy and interesting time. Staying in Booth Hall Hospital, an old isolation hospital near her home in Blackley, brought back memories of her treatment there for a broken arm. She had fallen, running in the school playground, and complained of pain. She was only eight years old, so her father, a good GP, was still around. Uncle Robert had come for supper with Auntie Serena and her cries were ignored by two doctors as they sat round the table eating. The next day, her father took her to Booth Hall for a checkup. Lo and behold, a green stick fracture was seen on x-ray. This occurs in children when the bone only splinters partly and has to be broken properly before it can be set. So, she ended up in the theatre.

We students would sit in front of the x-ray boxes viewing our first provisionally diagnosed case of scurvy. This vitamin C deficiency is recognised by evidence of bleeds beneath the linings of the bones in the arm and legs. It was a mystery how such a deficiency could occur in Manchester at that time when orange juice was freely distributed; had the mother, who was a Jamaican immigrant, boiled the orange juice in error?

This misdiagnosis turned out to be one of the first cases of child abuse seen in the hospital. The subperiosteal bleeds were due to trauma. The denials of the parents were convincing at first until the social workers took over and leached out a confession that they had bashed the infant.

So began the era of child abuse awareness in England. The first significant cases went on file in a children's home in Liverpool with twenty-six children aged six to sixteen in 1965. The housemaster was found guilty of buggery (the offence of rape did not exist then). Child abuse was described in 1962 by the American Medical Association. Within ten years, every state had statutes for mandatory reporting. The UK followed suit. The '70s revealed wife abuse. Elder abuse hit the headlines in the '90s and also became a statutory offence followed by sex abuse in the new millennium. A lot of these horrors happened in the home. Now the world is battling with paedophilia, snuff movies, and grooming, often leading to child kidnapping and even slavery. Misuse of and addiction to the internet by perverts is blamed. The television celebrity Jimmy Saville shocked the nation in 2015 when his crimes came to light; even in the mortuary, he could not resist his evil inclination.

While living at Pendlebury Children's Hospital, she met Tibor, an engineer, through Marietta, her Hungarian friend. He was a lonely 1956 refugee from Budapest; he became a friend and gave her bridge lessons. He was tall and dark with a rather large nose. His deep, chocolatey voice heavy with the Magyar accent came to haunt her down the years. He made her a delicious birthday cake, a musical box, the cherries lit up; it played "Tales from the Vienna Woods," a culinary engineer's delight, it was so complex. Before the birthday, he left cards saying so many weeks towards the surprise.

On the night, he drove her miles out into the Cheshire countryside to Nantwich. He slowed down. She was astonished to see a sign posted on the side of the road, fifty miles to Ethel's surprise, twenty miles to the surprise, and so on. It seemed romantic at the time, so much trouble for her. They had dinner in an Elizabethan manor and drove back through the darkened lanes, a long way home. It was 1:30 in the morning as she put the key in the door, but she was not prepared for the ferocious outburst of "Putane! Putane!" from Rex, who ran down the stairs to greet her in a red, snarling fury. He went out in his pyjamas and opened the car door. "How dare you bring her home so late?" he shouted at Tibor, who just smiled knowingly, probably guessing the jealousy that lay behind the whole scene. Rex had been waiting up for her, his imagination running wild. A sad, sick end to such an innocent evening of celebration.

Tibor's attention became oppressive; he would be waiting for her as she came out of Manchester Royal Infirmary casualty at night. She had been learning how to stitch; she wasn't sorry that her first attempt was the scalp of a German au pair, albeit under local anaesthetic, of course. He seemed to be everywhere she went, popping up, even in the morning when she left the house, despite him living on the other side of town twenty miles away; it was spooky. And she became fearful, telling him to cool it, to no avail.

On the train to London to visit a girlfriend, he suddenly appeared in the carriage and ended up escorting her around the West End, taking her to a Hungarian restaurant, the Gay Hussar. He misinterpreted a move to the powder room once at a party, hitting her in frustration as he thought she was leaving him. She shook him off eventually. Years of anonymous calls stalked her. Even when she got engaged twelve years later, he telephoned to congratulate her saying in his strong accent, "I will ring you when you get divorced," which he did! Only British Telecom finally squashed him for her, by blocking the calls.

It was coming up to finals, three weeks of daily exams, written, vivas, and practicals. They had to take a history, examine the patient, and present them to the examiner with the presumptive diagnosis. She had a case of multiple sclerosis. Rex came up trumps, driving her in each morning. She returned exhausted and feverish each evening but managed to get through the ordeal. Her father had diagnosed Crohn's disease on account of these fevers with bowel problems. Despite negative tests, she remained convinced for years that she harboured this malady.

Marietta was supposed to ring her with the results, and she waited in vain, jumping on the bus at the end herself and arriving to see crowds surging around the notice board. Her name was there, relief. She travelled back home to a similar low-key response as when she'd passed A-Levels.

Determined to celebrate somehow, she invited Robert and Serena to a dinner dance together with her parents. They tried to be nice, nevertheless, as they danced only together. She felt a mutt sitting there on her own.

A bitter postscript was Rex's manipulation to prevent her from attending graduation by insisting, "She needed a holiday before starting house jobs." The trip was booked to coincide with that date, so she sat on the balcony of the hotel in Riccione, disappointed at missing that moment of glory when she would wear a cap and gown. When she got back, she hired the mortar board and gown and went to have her photo taken. She remained resentful for a long time afterwards, seeing how other parents shared the joy of that occasion with their children and she had missed out. Many, many years later, on the graduation day of her daughter, Rex stopped her mother from attending, claiming her blood pressure was too high. She wondered if it was because he had graduated alone in Paris.

Chapter 8
Learning—A Lifelong Process

Hope Hospital in Eccles was her first house job. A fierce initiation. She was given a room in the doctors' residency, its walls made of chipboard dividing them from the tyranny of their neighbor's telephone, ringing throughout the night.

The food, horrific, the worst of British, justifying the phrase semantic void. "Bon appétit" is in French; the equivalent did not exist in English as the food was so bad. Black mutton and lumpy mash sat dismally on the dinner plates. Nowadays, British cuisine is improving, so "Enjoy your meal" is becoming the vernacular.

It was quite a walk over to the hospital in all weathers, as they were on call twenty-four hours at a time. A story circulated of a guy called to casualty in the middle of the night; when he didn't appear, the nurse rang him again and he promised to come. He was still a no-show, so they sent a porter to his room with a key. The young doctor was fast asleep with a telephone clutched to each ear.

Directed to the busy laundry fizzling from the steam, she was fitted with a white coat and together with her shiny new reflex hammer and tuning fork, she put her stethoscope in her pocket and found the ward appointed to her. It was a tame and pleasant beginning as she was introduced to the consultant, her boss for the next six months, Dr Walker, a tall, kindly young man, then her registrar, Dr Bradley, a small, plump woman who would be supervising her. She joined the ward round familiar from student days but this time in the capacity of one of the staff.

The "monster" arrived, the senior house officer, Dr Wilton, a pale, innocuous-looking bloke. She reckoned he was ex nostrils (Jewish). That first day progressed amicably.

The difficulty arose the first night she was on call for casualty duty. A man was brought in unconscious, and she had no idea how to cope alone in that situation. As a man's life was more important than her pride, she rang Dr Wilton for help. He came, hissing at her between his teeth. "Did you have to wake me? Couldn't you do it yourself?" He scowled; she felt inadequate and foolish.

She learnt about the important management of an unconscious patient that night, and it stood her in good stead for the rest of her medical life. A quick history from family to exclude trauma, epilepsy, or infection is to be taken. Drug history was vital to exclude overdose. Examination, especially neurological to assess level of coma or presence of meningitis, was part of this acute work. Urgent blood tests to estimate glucose, and other metabolites, not forgetting drug levels, if appropriate, had to be done. They were expected to learn on the job, as they knew next to nothing from a practical point of view. This approach characterised how she practised medicine; she was never afraid to ring for help even if it meant bothering a consultant or professor in the night.

The weeks rushed by. On her weekends on call, she'd be working Friday, Friday night, Saturday, Saturday night,

Sunday, Sunday night. Monday at 5:30 p.m. she drove home in her parents' old Morris Oxford, which she had bought for £200, to collapse into sleep. No shift work then.

One day, a diabetic woman came in; they established that she had had a heart attack and admitted her to the ward. Ethel's lovely registrar was not on duty that day; she had to handle it alone. She took the history, got the list of antidiabetic drugs from the relatives, and treated her with oxygen and the appropriate cardiac therapy.

However, the patient slipped slowly into a coma, suffered cardiac shock, and died. Dr Bradley reappeared the next day and discovered that she had not taken her antidiabetic drugs on the morning she took ill.

Ethel was totally broken, thinking she had been remiss in her care, sure she had caused her death. When she got home that night, Rex was comforting. He said, "If you are a general you are responsible for many lives if you make a mistake. If you are a bus driver, the same." She was a little mollified, but it took a long time before she stopped going through private postmortems over the deaths of her patients.

Subsequent research showed that cardiac shock in severely obese diabetics had a bad prognosis, most of them dying.

One evening, she rang the telephonist in the hospital to put her through to her home, who said, "Have you heard the news?"

"No."

"President Kennedy has been assassinated."

Nearly everyone alive at that time remembers what they were doing when they heard that news. It was a shock to learn that such a charismatic young celebrity was mortal and died so violently, his glamorous wife, Jackie, by his side. She had faced the peaceful reality of death in the dissecting room and on the simultaneous death of her beloved grandfather but still, the vulnerability of this strong character brought the fact home with a jolt.

Another shock was a phone call from Margaret, her old school friend.

"Have you heard the news?" "No."

"Tom is engaged; I read it in *The Jewish Chronicle*."

This blow actually gave her an acute stress peptic ulcer as evidenced by sharp indigestion and pain; her own diagnosis. It healed over the weeks but she was able to observe on herself what trauma, even a severe burn, can do. This was in a way a self-inflicted fire. Her first love was gone forever. The path ahead was empty and never restocked at that level. She just had to carry on.

The period of the '60s was permeated by the Beatles' music. Even now, on hearing the song "I Want to Hold Your Hand," it takes her back to dancing at parties in the mess and her love-hate dependence on Dr Wilton. Uphill moments had occurred when her ignorance irritated him. He'd roll his eyes at her and she grew to be a little afraid of him. Her innate sense of inferiority brought out the bully in him. Nevertheless, she needed his help and support, and she did fancy him a little.

The medical staff would meet for a free drug lunch, which consisted of sandwiches bought in a supermarket, talk to the reps about their new products, and then going into the lecture theatre. It also gave an opportunity to discuss difficult cases with other disciplines. She was asked to present her successful diagnosis of Polyarteritis Nodosa at the weekly meeting. She was nervous, of course, but managed to paint a picture of the auto immune disease in a man suffering from red nodules on his legs and general flu-like symptoms. Afterwards, she was chuffed to be told by Dr Bradley, "That was masterly." Wilton left the room without saying a word. It was her swan song for Hope Hospital.

She was happy to have had her next post in the teaching hospital, Manchester Royal Infirmary, a surgical house job in the Ear, Nose, and Throat department under Prof L. Strangely. He had treated her as a four-year-old during the war for deafness following a middle ear infection, when she was one of the earliest to receive sulphonamide, the first antibacterial discovered in the '30s by Domagk, who was forced to refuse the Nobel Prize by the Nazis. Prof L. was old now and sometimes his shaking hand had to be steadied while he operated.

A throwback to Victorian times was the separate dining room for lady doctors from the men. The food was better; she especially enjoyed the cheese, biscuits, and celery served after each meal. The long, open, draughty corridors of the old hospital, though, were tiresome at night.

The routine of clerking in new patients and doing audiograms was broken by occasional heart-lurching situations.

One day, about to leave sister's office, she came up close to Ethel. A slim, dark woman, smiling, she fingered her dress, "Nice material," she said. Ethel suddenly remembered a rumour of lesbianism and, realising why she was always so nice, she made her escape. It was yet another aspect of community life to be experienced.

That year, being away from home for the first time, working as a doctor, was daunting. The overriding fear of failing the patient was the constant.

Chapter 9
London at Last

The General Medical Council document of full registration arrived one morning, after completing the second of two compulsory preregistration house jobs at her alma mater. Now, she could go to London, her original plan, thwarted by her stepfather.

She was delighted to obtain a rotating senior house officer post at Queen Elizabeth Hospital for Children in Hackney Road, starting at Queen Mary's Hospital in Carshalton, Surrey. Paediatrics was her chosen specialty at that time, and it was exciting to get such a good post.

Marietta, her medic friend, planned to drive with her down to London because she was starting a new job in Hackney as well. However, it was foggy that Sunday. Marietta's father thought it was too dangerous to drive and sent her in the train. Later, she described a gorgeous boy she had met on that train, her eyes sparkling.

She waited awhile, but the fog did not lift. Rex said she should fulfill her commitments and must go. The motorways were reasonably clear, but driving down the dark, misty, strange country lanes of Surrey was frightening. When she found herself on the wrong side of the road, she mentally cursed her stepfather for putting her into such a dangerous situation, even questioning his motive. She did arrive safely and settled quickly into that lovely area.

The cystic fibrosis wards were her brief; it was tragic to see these babies and their elders growing up into the angry, chronically sick, many of them not surviving past teenage years. Nowadays, they survive into their forties or more thanks to lung transplants and new treatments.

The first known reference is a Scandinavian folklore adage: "Woe to that child which, when kissed on the forehead tastes salty. He is bewitched and soon must die." The saying refers to the salty sweat that is the basis of the diagnosis. It is a recessive genetic disease affecting cell membrane conductance. The thick secretion in the lungs leads to frequent pneumonia, abnormal sweat, and pancreatic atrophy, resulting in loss of the enzyme required for normal digestion.

Accurate physiotherapy leading to good drainage of the lung was taught to the parents. Nebulisers and antibiotics, as necessary, were the basic treatments as well as pancreatic replacement therapy. Nowadays, lung transplants can help.

The medical staff visited the main Hackney hospital for meetings, where she came across the registrar Jo Miller, a dynamic, wiry young man apparently well-loved and respected. One weekend, he dropped into Carshalton when she was on duty, as he said his parents lived nearby.

Pleased, she referred indirectly to their common background by mentioning Israel; he took the hint and asked her out.

At the end of their first date at Rules, the famous restaurant, she offered to go Dutch. He demurred, saying that her task was to look as good as possible for the date. He said this so nicely that she was not hurt at all and always remembered that her contribution was to take special care of getting ready for future encounters.

Flattered and happy to be his companion, she went with him to a Spike Milligan show; they had all been *Goon Show* fans at school, glued to the radio in their teenage years. She was really enjoying London as much as she had hoped.

Jo suggested they break up. She agreed, and choked inside. She began work at the more challenging acute children's hospital in Hackney. They pretended not to know each other; she thought he was ashamed, fearing she could not handle the pressure.

After watching her out of the corner of his eye, putting up intravenous drips into neonates' scalps at three in the morning—"Dripping time," he called it—he asked to come back. It was one of her happiest times. Lots of good mess social life, going to the pub off duty, to the Good Friends Chinese. Getting to know London, its thirty-three Wren churches and the East End. The Seekers' song "I Know I'll Never Find Another You" is still evocative of Jo.

She was learning paediatrics, her favourite work so far. The way the babies were brought into casualty, so ill and shocked with meningitis or bronchiolitis, and recovered so quickly with the right treatment. Seeing a bonny smiling infant the next morning was a joy.

The opposite could happen; a colleague sent a baby home, thinking it healthy enough, to be faced with a sobbing mother bringing her lifeless daughter back the next day.

Churchill died; she walked down Whitehall with Jo in the dark and joined the long queue to see the great man lying in state. It was something momentous, the solemn marching past, and she felt part of history.

She was still innocent in physical relationships, and Jo respected this completely. They would lie together, hug, and kiss, but nothing more ever tempted her at that time. In retrospect, she supposed she just did not fancy him enough.

The Eichmann trial was still proceeding from April 1961. One morning at breakfast, the senior registrar, who lived at home, came in saying, "The Israelis are right to stage this show trial; it's a revelation to me." He had known nothing about the Holocaust. Of course, this was one of the reasons Israel was put on trial. Youngsters everywhere were growing up unaware of the horrors of the Shoah. Later, Margaret Thatcher changed this by making it part of the school curriculum.

Eichmann had presided over the murder of millions and was unapologetic right to the end. Even in the last year of the war, he was sent to Hungary and said, "If it's the last thing I do, I will clean Hungary of all its Jews." He did this easily as birth certificates there identified "Jew," so they were rounded up from towns and villages quickly and marched to concentration camps for slaughter. She much later visited many beautifully coloured, wooden, empty synagogues in towns all over Hungary. Afterwards, Eichmann transformed himself into a nondescript Ricardo Klement and lived in Argentina, incognito till 1960.

In May 1960, David Ben-Gurion, prime minister of Israel, announced in the Knesset that Mossad had kidnapped Eichmann in Buenos Aires and brought him to Israel. The Israeli ambassador in Buenos Aires was declared persona non grata and deported.

“A watershed in Israeli history, made possible only by the existence of a sovereign state of the Jews,” said Ben-Gurion. Four hundred journalists arrived in Israel, and the Shoah was caught in the headlights of international media interest.

Eichmann was executed by hanging in 1962, the only case of corporal punishment in modern Israeli history. In the time of the temple, even the High Priest, while officiating, could be taken to stand trial for murder.

Ethel had been steeped in the narrative. At age five, she had found a thin red book in her grandfather’s bureau; *News Chronicle* was printed on the front. She opened it to see photographs of skeletal cadaverous people on one page, just skulls or lampshades on another. She gazed, uncomprehending but horrified; she closed the lid of the bureau and crept to bed.

Her stepfather, always brooding over books about different aspects of that terrible time, influenced her teenage years. He was looking for news of his mother and sisters, who had disappeared from Lodz, Poland without a trace. He was racked with guilt because he had left them alone, to study in Paris, and never went back to check up on them. He had also refused to marry a friend, in a ruse to get her out of Poland; her subsequent death lay heavily on his conscience. A cousin in Israel gave a lecture to the synagogue recently, proving that the figure of six million slaughtered in the Shoah was wrong. He had proof from newly discovered mass graves that the true number was nearer ten million.

Marietta, her Manchester friend, was at the nearby Homerton Hospital so they went back to Manchester together to visit their parents. One evening, she turned up at their house in Blackley to tell her she was engaged to the guy she had met on the train. Ethel was so happy for her; she opened the bottle of champagne, which was a qualifying present, and they drank to the celebration.

After she had gone home, Rex stormed in beetroot-faced and screaming "monkey, monkey," waving his arms round and round under his armpits, more like a monkey than he knew. "Why make a fool of yourself like that?" Deflated and bowed, she realised he was jealous in some distorted way for her.

She was getting overtired, and by the end of this post, her old fevers and tummy upsets surfaced, reinforcing her fears of Crohn's disease, which her father had erroneously diagnosed.

The parents appeared at the hospital and insisted she go back home with them. "It's all too much for you; it's making you ill." She followed them back to Manchester up the M1, her heart heavy. Part of her knew their possessiveness was reclaiming her into their clutches. Rex had nastily called her Jo "a coat hanger," his envy exposed.

Jo understood; he sent a bouquet of red roses and a letter saying, "Whatever happens, she must return to London and get herself away." She had doubts about Jo as a long-term partner because she knew that his father may have been a depressive, a hereditary disease. However, his advice was good. She needed to get out.

This was not the end of her London adventure. She began applying for posts in London.

Chapter 10
Climbing the Ladder 1965–1970

"Drive down Regent Street and turn left at the Café Royal!" Those were the directions to reach her next job at the Royal National Throat, Nose and Ear Hospital in Golden Square. It sounded romantic: she was relieved to be leaving Manchester again after a period, cooped up, whilst looking for a post, and determined to get back to London. Golden Square is beautiful with a touch of Amsterdam to its surrounding old buildings, each so different in architecture from its neighbour. The hospital mess was high up in the eaves, and the living room looked out on the square.

Nearby was Carnaby Street, symbol of the swinging '60s where the youth, liberated by the new oral contraceptive, enjoyed the music of the Rolling Stones and the Beatles in the Marquess club. Trendy fashions, such as those by Mary Quant, added to the frenetic cocktail. Even menswear transited to bold colours. Her hair was done at Vidal Sassoon in Bond Street, notable for its clients crying at the washroom mirrors, reflecting their shorn, jagged look.

Raymond's Revue Bar, notorious for the Profumo affair, was around the corner, but Mandy Rice Davies, the celebrity prostitute, had long gone to Israel to marry. It was thrilling walking around Brewer Street, Soho with its exotic restaurants, delis, and Floris, the chocolate shop, not to mention the strip bars with dicey-looking blokes hanging outside.

She was toying with the idea of doing ENT as her permanent speciality, and this job would be decisive. They were attached to the main hospital in Gray's Inn Road.

One evening, a documentary on television was showing how the British sent back the illegal ships, bringing Holocaust survivors to Palestine, then a British Mandate. Ernest Bevin had ignored a Labour Party vote to rescind the White Paper of 1939, allowing only 75,000 Jews to immigrate to Palestine in five years (both Lloyd George and Churchill had voted against). The illegal immigrants were sent back to Germany or detained in camps in Cyprus. The internees included many children and orphans.

A pukka anaesthetist was watching with her. "I was there as a major," he said in his polished accent. "I enjoyed sending those ships back." He grinned.

"I am Jewish," she replied. He paled and quickly disappeared from the room; after that he treated her carefully.

Another anti-Semitic episode occurred. A Robert Redford look-alike, a classy young surgeon, came into the residency with a piece of nasal cartilage he had removed during an operation. "I can make you a Jewish nose," he joked. He didn't realise that she was Jewish, or did he? She never experienced such behaviour again.

The routine of clerking in patients was broken by occasional heart-lurching situations. Standing in the theatre, a crisis develops when the patient turns blue and the anaesthetist is unsure of the cause. She rushes out to obtain an urgent portable x-ray that reveals a pneumothorax or air in the chest cavity, which in turn presses on the lung, squeezing it. A needle was put in and the air hissed out. Watching it bubble through a drain into a bottle was a wonderful relief to them all.

She learnt to take out tonsils and adenoids and wash out sinuses; it was a perk to have her own surgical list. On one occasion, she performed a drainage operation on the sinuses called a Caldwell-Luc, a complicated procedure. Why was it allowed, albeit under supervision?

A realisation came that surgery was not for her; all that anatomy to study again, as well as the effect of premenstrual tension on one's surgical ability.

She went through a few different jobs after this, returning to her real love, paediatrics, as SHO at West Middlesex Hospital, and even tried dermatology at St John's Hospital for Skin Diseases, following in her dad's footsteps, working on photosensitivity in porphyria patients. However, she had to leave hastily after developing an eye hypersensitivity to the light machine she was working with, sans special protective goggles.

On June 5, 1967, the Six-Day War broke out in Israel. Nasser had received a false report from the Soviet Union that Israel was massing on its borders, so he reacted by building up his own forces there, also blocking the straits of Tiran again to ships bound for Israel, as in 1956. Nowadays, this would be an example of fake news causing a war.

Egyptian forces crossed the Suez Canal into Sinai and also made a pact with Jordan and Syria. Abba Eban, the Israeli foreign minister, came to Britain in a futile attempt to avoid war. Israel had no choice but to respond to the massive buildup of Arab forces along its borders. Israel launched an attack of airfields, destroying 350 Egyptian airplanes on the ground as well as 29 Iraqi and 150 Syrian planes in all.

Jordan entered the suburb of Armon Hanaziv in Jerusalem, despite promising Israel it would not attack. There was a ferocious battle in Ammunition Hill with many brave casualties. This was decisive in allowing Israeli defence forces to gain access to the old city and the Wailing Wall, a huge emotional achievement for Jews everywhere. It was the only remaining site of the second temple and led to the reunification of a divided Jerusalem.

In the meantime, Syria attacked from the Golan Heights in the north, where a hairy battle took place; hundreds of Syrian tanks against a handful of Israeli ones. An absolute miracle it was, and most of us truly believe that the hand of G-d was present. Eli Cohen, the spy, had helped by manipulating the Syrians to plant trees over spots, marking their underground bunkers.

In six days, Israel pushed Jordan out of Jerusalem and Syria from the Golan Heights. She regained Sinai once again too.

Ethel drove to Manchester for the weekend. When Rex got nasty about her yellow armchair Zionism, he blanched as she told him that she had come specially to say goodbye, before volunteering to go and help.

Anyhow, she was told they did not need her; Israel had too many volunteers. She felt ashamed of her relief, even though she had wanted to go.

The Member of the Royal College of Physicians diploma was the next hurdle in the professional rat race, so a post as registrar in geriatric medicine at Whittington Hospital was ideal for its excellent teaching course.

She was living in the Highgate flat, which her parents had bought for ten thousand pounds in 1967. The monies had been obtained from the sale of Glaxo shares originally invested at two thousand pounds. The value of the flat jumped enormously in line with everything else, so in 2012, she could sell it for £400,000. No wonder it whetted her appetite for playing with the stock market, her hobby ever since.

As a registrar in geriatric medicine at Whittington Hospital from 1967 to '69, she began to experience the curious effects of propinquity.

The hospital was situated on Highgate Hill, where a glass case containing Dick Whittington's cat (a stuffed replica) disclosed the spot where the bells of London sang, "Turn again, Whittington, lord mayor of London."

Working closely with male colleagues, she would get attached to one of them. Long ward rounds; eating meals together, running to emergencies and coping with them. Then sharing the relief or disappointment of the aftermath led to a bonding. Waves of attraction would gather over her.

This happened first with an Indian SHO, Sam Mani. His broad smile and solid demeanour charmed her. Nothing ever happened.

Then came Paul O'Connell, an Irish failed priest who had escaped seduction at his seminary to become a doctor. Highly intelligent, he helped her with physiology studies for the part-one exam for the MRCP diploma; he was her senior house officer.

His deep Irish brogue, she can hear it now. Twinkling eyes and again a certain solidity of form beguiled her, and they became friends. He visited her in the new flat with its turquoise blue leather sofas, where an adolescent physical relationship began, but went nowhere.

He also hurt her in subtle ways, by flirting with talented lady doctors; explained, when she noticed suddenly that he fancied the naked man stretched out on the bed, surrounded by postgraduate students, on a teaching round. His eyes were glued to the guy's pelvis.

Again, at the tea table in the mess, she became aware that Paul was similarly attracted to a swarthy, young houseman. Flushed, his pupils dilated, and licking his lips, he couldn't take his eyes off the unsuspecting hero. It was a flash of revelation to observe this happening. He admitted to her that he had these leanings, a residue of his time in the seminary.

However, they remained somehow involved with each other, though it could be painful. At her wedding ceremony in 1973 in Manchester, she looked up to see him in the gallery, his head and body falling, fainting and stressed.

He married an Irish girl, had two boys, and settled in Dublin. She rang him once on a visit to Ireland. He greeted her: "I thought you were dead."

Whittington was an alarming and challenging job that she enjoyed thoroughly. She ran day or night to crash calls. Faced with difficult cases, sometimes solved by a visit to the hospital library at night as registrar on call, she was responsible for the whole caboodle.

Ethel had to be a barrister for a pregnant woman, brought in with carbon monoxide poisoning, by pleading her case for a place in the high-pressure oxygen chamber at University College Hospital. It was a triumph to get her transferred there.

One morning, she came to the ward to the tragic news that the son and daughter-in-law of the ward sister had been gassed by a faulty heater, emitting carbon monoxide. Landlords were not prepared to pay for the servicing of these radiators; now it is statutory.

There for two years, she studied at home advanced physiology. As a group of young medics in the same boat, they helped each other, going over old papers and discussing problems together. The advantage of attending the Membership course was a boon too.

She passed part one of the Membership exam; her parents happened to be staying on a visit from Manchester. She remembers hearing the envelope drop through the letterbox onto the floor. These achievements are moments of joy. They all went out to Highgate village for lunch and her stepfather made a toast to part two, which she thought was pouring cold water over the glory.

Whittington Hospital, part of an old workhouse, was divided into three wings spreading across two main roads. She was doing a ward round, where the sister occasionally went around with a stick hitting the men in a strategic place if she suspected them of self-abuse. She glanced at the television; she heard the magical words, "A giant leap for mankind," and behold, there were men walking on the moon! This was 1969 just before she left and marked the end of a momentous period.

The next post was in paediatrics and medicine at Elizabeth Garret Anderson Hospital in Euston Road, now a fire station, named after the first lady doctor to graduate from the Royal Free Hospital, renowned for women students. Ethel touted herself all over London in order to attend the famous teaching rounds for the clinical part two of the MRCP exam. The Royal National Hospital for Nervous Diseases, Charing Cross Hospital in Hyde Park corner, now the Langham hotel. They were expected to know the huge textbook of diseases, and these teaching rounds were a way of seeing very rare maladies presented to us in depth such as Huntingdon's chorea.

She even attended the notorious Dr Papworth's lectures and studied his bible, *A Primer of Medicine*. He was a small, vibrant maverick who separated himself from the establishment, saying he refused to be a human sigmoidoscope, implying he was no sycophant and possibly incorruptible. He taught them to be really excellent clinicians; she will always be grateful to him for pulling up her standard to the required level. At a private lesson in his Harley St place, she was distressed when he made a pass, smirking up at her with wandering hands.

The exam came around; she passed the clinical but failed the viva. One of the things she didn't know was the commonest cause of death in young people—road traffic accidents.

Eventually, she got through part two and gained her MRCP in 1970. Her mother came down for the ceremony at the wonderful modern Royal College of Physicians in Regent's Park. It was especially good to share this happy occasion with the mum who had encouraged her all the way. They had also missed out on the last graduation, making this one doubly enjoyable. Rex stayed in Manchester.

Her next ambition was to get the MRS and qualify as a wife.

Chapter 11
Israel on Immigrant Status

Her membership of the Royal College of Physicians in the bag, what to do next?

A mother's influence was behind her choice of skin diseases, saying it was a more feminine attractive speciality than geriatrics. Also, as her father had worked in Israel in the dermatology department, she had some "protecsia" in clinching a job in that prestigious teaching hospital, where she could achieve her growing desire to settle in Israel, the proper place for Jews. She felt British but a visitor here in England, at the same time.

She wrote, enclosing her CV, to Hadassah hospital in Jerusalem, where her dad had worked, when he left her aged eleven years in 1951. Professor Zagher, head of the Department of Dermatology, accepted her as a first assistant. She was delighted and so began the process of "Aliyah" (Going Up), the term used for immigrating to Israel, implying a spiritual ascent.

Israel had "The Law of Return," which accepts any Jew into their rightful place there. The London branch of the Jewish Agency did the assessing of suitability, requiring her to attend many interviews and go through much bureaucracy.

Eventually, she found herself, one sunny morning, in Auntie Gilda's car being driven to the airport to embark on an exciting new phase.

Not arriving as a tourist felt different and nerve-racking. Was she being foolhardy? After being welcomed by Aliyah officials in their airport office, and given a "teudah," a temporary passport, entitling her to certain rights, she felt better. This new identity gave her a recognised status.

She was allocated to an absorption centre, a hostel called Bet Giora in a suburb of Jerusalem, a mountainous bus ride from Hadassah hospital. Her room was seven feet wide with a cold shower, which she endured for eighteen months.

The inmates were friendly, families from the world over struggling to come to terms with their ambivalent situation; joy to be in the "Promised Land" but grim at the realities of life there, and probably suffering from culture shock simultaneously. That is the story of immigrants.

It was February, the time of "New Year for Trees," the beginning of the ancient tax year and the first signs of spring. Pink and white almond blossoms flourished everywhere on the roadside. It reminds her of A. E. Houseman's poem, "Loveliest of Trees the Cherry Now." A few weeks later, the fields are dotted with red and blue anemones, and sweet, clean-smelling yellow acacia trees line the roads. It really is the best time to be in Israel.

The newly built Hadassah lay in the valley of Ein Kerem, the spot chosen by Ben-Gurion, after the original hospital, founded in 1939 on Mount Scopus, was closed down in the War of Independence in 1948. The day after independence was declared, the Arabs attacked from all fronts. A convoy of doctors and nurses bringing medical supplies to that hospital was ambushed. Seventy-nine were massacred by Arab forces despite being escorted by Haganah militia.

Chagall made Hadassah hospital famous by agreeing to design the most beautiful stained-glass windows for the synagogue, cobalt blues, carmine red, all colours of the rainbow in a stunning splash!

The department was welcoming; some even remembered her father. The hurdle was the language. She attended an ulpan three times a week, set up for medical staff in Bet Giora. Dr Gold, who became her mentor and her adoptive family, suggested she get a notebook and write down ten new words a day in Hebrew. Breakthrough advice, it was. Jargon for any new job is apparently about five hundred words, so she was soon able to talk to her patients in "broken chocolate" Hebrew. Inevitable howlers followed, her telling a patient to take off his trousers (michnasaim) instead of glasses (mishkafaim). Calling the head nurse wicked (rashait) instead of head (rashit) wasn't helpful.

She even insulted an Arab patient by asking him to bring three specimens of chara, which she thought meant stool but actually means "shit." They laughed together, once explained. This test was very important, as a lot of the skin ailments were caused by parasites and worms, and some patients had a zoo in their specimens.

Traditionally, the world over, dermatology goes with venereology. However, in her medical school, women students were not allowed to attend the sexually transmitted diseases clinics. This was probably a throwback to Victorian prudery. So naturally, she begged off that side of the work, until the arrival of a South African lady doctor, who went pouting to the professor, saying it was not fair.

In actual fact, after an initial shrinking, she rather enjoyed dealing with the hippies carrying at least two nasty visitors, one of which might be lice or scabies. She must say, she learnt a lot.

One day, the professor called us all in to see a yeshiva boy. He was sitting up on the examination couch in his religious garb but trouser-less, his beard and long side locks betraying his strict background. They gathered round as the professor demonstrated their first case of syphilis, pointing out the chancre or ulcer on his penis.

Suddenly, the examining professor noticed something and shouted out, “A tsitsus! A tsitsus!” He was referring to the long white fringes of the ritual bodice the seminarian was required to wear. She is laughing now as she writes; it was so funny, reminding her of “A handbag!” in Oscar Wilde’s play *The Importance of Being Earnest*. The lad was admitted to the ward and treated with penicillin. He told his visiting rabbis that he had a hernia; nobody questioned it.

Another time, Professor Zagher came to her with a patient’s notes saying, “This is your father’s handwriting in perfect Hebrew.” She was touched. Her daddy had studied at a yeshiva in Vilna, in Yiddish, which is written in Hebrew script.

Her London cousin Isabel and her husband Rotem lived nearby in Bayit Vegan. They gave her wonderful support throughout. Rotem was a fascinating character, a fifth-generation Sabra, a vibrant academic in Middle Eastern studies, and a lieutenant colonel in the Israeli Army.

He would turn up with his young children on a Friday and whisk her from her little room to a picnic in the Jerusalem

Forest or to join him in supermarket shopping. This was vital in making her feel at home in a new country.

A seminal event in her life occurred, whilst she was staying with them over the Sabbath. He noticed that she had locked the door of the room she had been sleeping in, and remarked on it. She had felt it was the norm. He took her out onto the balcony into the bright sunshine and began by saying, "It was not as normal as she thought." Gently, he elicited out of her depth the reason behind this behaviour, her stepfather's predatory actions. This was the first time in her life, at the age of thirty-one, that she had spoken of such things. It was releasing; Rotem also explained to her that Rex's cruel teasing was a response to her rejecting him. A clever revelation. Slowly, Israel was maturing her and solving some of her life puzzles.

The summer arrived, those days so hot she would crawl off the bus, buy a large bottle of grapefruit drink and a *Jerusalem Post* at the kiosk, then stagger into her room; just couldn't wait to drink down the bottle in huge gulps to quench that thirst.

Shabat could be lonely when she wasn't invited and she'd wander around the empty little square of Kiryat Hayovel and eat in one of the small cafés, a kebab with a tasty Israeli salad of finely chopped tomatoes, cucumbers, and peppers.

An invitation came to meet other medical "olim chadashim" (new immigrants) at the doctors' house in Strauss Street.

There she met a reddish-haired charming Persian, B, named after a great king of the fifth century, said to have had a Jewish mother, Shushandukht. Ethel was charmed by this tall, slim obstetrician working at the nearby Bikur Cholim hospital as he smilingly chatted her up.

One early June evening, he took her for a magical walk between tall Cypress and Pine trees at the side of Mount Herzl. The fragrances of the trees' resins, the shrill cicadas, and the view dropping away into the village of Ein Karem in the valley below imprinted the impossible friendship upon her like a mirage. She met his brother and cousin, both doctors, in fact his very surname; Pezeshk meant doctor in Farsi.

She and he took a carefree trip down to the Dead Sea, munching a huge bowl of blood-red watermelon. The blow fell by the freshwater springs, when she caught him flirting playfully with a girl in their group. It hurt, as she absorbed the shock in the ladies' washroom.

Late for a date one evening, she called him from the phone box. He bade her, "Don't come! I will see you tomorrow."

Driven by wild feelings inside, she called a cab and chased up Ramat Eshcol to his newly built flat. She knocked, looked through the letter box and could see a girl running from the bedroom to the bathroom. He let her in, showing her a box of pistachios which he said she had brought from Teheran, a gift from his parents.

He ushered the girl out. Ethel vomited in the toilet. The upheaval and disappointment took its toll. Of course, she shouldn't have gone. It hadn't helped that she was a professional virgin, well indoctrinated by her stepfather, whose shadow still loomed over her. B's loss of face spelt the end. She chased him a few times to no avail. She had sabotaged her own happiness again.

On a drug-sponsored weekend to the Dead Sea, she made two lifelong friends, Nadia and Itta. The plug was that the ointment, made from the black mud there, cured psoriasis. Nadia was a young doctor. Itta was a Dutch nurse who had been hidden throughout the war by Righteous Gentiles in Holland. Tall, optimistic, strong, she had the gift of ESP and would forecast later as she drove her to the airport to go back to England that she would return with a husband and children.

A year into her stay, she was summoned to the warden's office and there, waiting, were two official men who asked her to sit down. They identified themselves as being from the shabak responsible for the Israeli internal intelligence. Visions of Mata Hari swam before her. They asked her if she was willing to lend her British passport for a while. A quandary: she knew that if she did anything illegal, she could lose her right to practise medicine altogether, but she did not want to appear a coward.

So, she temporised, telling them she needed to think about it, at the same time deciding to ask her guru, Rotem. He agreed, so she told them no.

The only time in her working medical life that she felt apprehensive of catching a disease was attending the leprosarium attached to a convent in Talpiot. Once, she had been impressed when her father had pointed to a passenger on the bus and whispered, "He has got leprosy."

The convent was situated in lovely gardens and was rumoured to have been involved in espionage goings-on by the nuns, contacting Germans and Turks in the past. They all sat around a big oak dining table together; she felt nervous but ate the food.

The patients, mostly Indian from Cochin, were thin and delicate. Leprosy was just becoming treatable with Dapsone, and these scarred people with depigmented patches were full of hope. Nowadays, it is Ethiopian immigrants who are the leprosy patients, but treated at home. The hospital is now a museum, converted by the leprosy nurse, a relative of mine. She works peripatetically treating the patients at home.

Ethel began to have doubts about dermatology altogether, especially after the professor called her to diagnose a strange-looking leg ulcer. She asked the patient a few questions about his general health, as taught in medical school; basic history taking. When he acknowledged that he had chest problems, she added two and two together and jumped to sarcoidosis as the cause of his ulcer.

"Correct," the irritated professor replied. "But for the wrong reasons. You should not take a history but recognise the disease as you would a Renoir or Rembrandt painting in an art gallery." This went against the whole grain of the art of medicine in her book, where taking a good history will give you the diagnosis at least fifty per cent of the time only to be verified by the examination. Nowadays, medics are spoilt by instant CT and MRI scans, which can make them lazy.

She enjoyed the detective hunt for the truth.

Also, she could not see a solution to her quest for a spouse at the age of thirty-one. She was waking in the morning with scratches on her nose, so torn was she with the decision whether to return to England. As became her wont, whenever she couldn't make a difficult judgement, she would wait a while and a third extraneous thing would appear to clinch it one way or another.

Betty, an acquaintance, had offered her place to share in Metudella Street. When she arrived, a neighbour had to let her in, telling her Betty had gone to Damascus for a visit—unheard of at that time. It felt weird being in someone's empty flat; it had been agreed, she told herself. The place was a mess, the bathroom filthy, especially the black bath. She cleaned it as well as she could and immersed herself.

Betty returned, bemused to find her there but accepting in her vague way. Then she noticed a nasty infection from her nether area. This frightened her; she assumed it was from the black bath, that she had not cleaned it adequately. Treatment with antibiotics from the hospital pharmacy soon cured her.

However, this prompted her to decide that she was going back to the UK. Parity was paramount!

Itta drove her to the airport. Eighteen months was all she had managed.

Chapter 12
Return to UK 1972

Back in London, the post of senior registrar in geriatric medicine at Central Middlesex Hospital fell into her hands. This was her true passion, the last of the general medical specialities; it also included skin, eyes, even some surgical problems as well as psychology and psychiatry.

She reckoned that her love and respect for her grandparents, whilst growing up in Southport, had fostered her enjoyment of the company of the aged, who had lived through two world wars and could be fascinating. People who threw their hands up in horror on hearing her choice were only threatened by old age themselves. A universal fear.

Driving daily from Highgate through the back of Willesden and Harlesden to the sprawling hospital in Park Royal became routine for the next two years. The hospital consisted of many old brick buildings over a few acres; it had a grim history when she arrived, the famous Dr A., father of Jane Asher, the film star, had committed suicide in his office followed by the suicide of a couple of house officers in the residency. The friendliness of everyone offset the rumour.

Ethel's Manchester mother had commiserated at a wedding with a Leeds mother who also had an unmarried offspring. They exchanged telephone numbers and that is how she got a call from Martin, a maths lecturer at Imperial, London University.

She declined his initial offer of a standing ticket at the opera, so he upgraded it to a balcony seat at the back. He welcomed her at Beth House behind the Albert Hall, where he was student warden, with excellent open sandwiches.

He was personable, interesting to talk to; she liked the picture on his wall, a Renoir. He was slim, bespectacled, and they got on well.

It was not love at first sight.

He sent her a postcard from a conference in Munich at a nerve-wracking time, 1972. The Summer Olympics were on; so was a massacre of eleven Israeli athletes, who were taken hostage and killed by Palestinian terrorists. She had to cancel a Hebrew lesson with an Israeli teacher, they were both so distraught. Over the years, each one of these Black September terrorists was sought and killed by Mossad agents in operation Wrath of God. There is a Steven Spielberg film, *Munich*, about it. Justice or revenge is questionable, but countering terrorism is paramount.

We started going out regularly. He was a bit cold; after she pointed this out, he said, "I will hold your hand because you asked me to." He would ride over to Highgate on his moped. They visited his old Cambridge college, she driving her old Morris. Eventually, she made some hint, and he followed it up in his flat by saying, "That is a proposal, if that's what you want."

She said, "Yes," and felt happy and flat at the same time, then rang her mum whose immediate reaction was, "No!"

Apparently, her mother and stepfather lay in bed the night she brought him home to Manchester saying, "He's not right." Rex replied, "If that's all she can find at thirty-two, better leave it."

Martin was a dead ringer for Woody Allen, slightly odd, showing the whites of his eyes when stressed, but brilliant, having written a book on stochastic processes. She felt he was right for her.

Later, psychotherapy revealed that she subconsciously chose a man who was not physical because of her fear of men, Rex.

The parents put her in a quandary by offering her a thousand pounds cash to forego a white wedding. The kindly spinster secretaries in the office were horrified and told her to go for it. She had waited so long.

Mother gave her hassle, her artistic superiority bridled at her wanting pink and yellow flowers for the wedding; but gave in to her "folie" after she got upset. It's now a common colour combination in fashion, still her favourite for flowers. Mother took over everything, even choosing the gifts in the wedding list since "Ethel was away in London." She was thus lumbered; she received lots of silver plate gallery trays.

Martin's parents came over to lunch in the new house in Prestwich. Rex had built it from a £25 ready plan and supervised the building. He called it Villa Tola after one of his sisters, lost to the Holocaust. It stood in a lovely garden of willows and circular rose beds. Beautiful, vivid flowered carpets, different in every room, were chosen by her mum and hoovered daily by the cleaner. All was friendly, until her stepfather suddenly announced at the table with a nasty sneer on his face, "She wants to marry in a white dress." John, Martin's father, a Dublin-trained doctor like her dad, ignored the comment but she was in a turmoil of righteous indignation. How could he? All those years of maintaining her virginity had passed, only to be falsely accused of this. What an unjust bastard. She had to grin and bear the humiliation.

She didn't realise till later that raw jealousy was behind the behaviour. Rex stopped her grandmother from taking her digoxin heart tablets just weeks before the wedding. The first news she had on returning from the honeymoon was that of her grandma's death of a silent myocardial infarction, common in diabetics. She had always said, "I want to live to see my granddaughter married." They had visited her in her flat, still in the wedding dress with her groom. It was a shocking homecoming for her. Needing to absorb the news and mourn in her own way, she asked Martin if he would switch off the television, explaining why. He refused, uncomprehending, probably thinking she was being bossy. She was forced to write "thank you" letters for the wedding gifts, at the table, with the screen blaring, which jarred with her emotional state. A bleak, lonely intro to married life. No loving care. With hindsight, maybe she was selfish too; she could have gone into the kitchen.

Her darkest suspicion of Rex's last sinister effort to abort the marriage by stopping grandma's medication, expediting her death, floated in her mind. She attempted to dismiss it as paranoia.

Whenever they visited Manchester in the years to come even with young children, he would disappear, and stay in his room the whole time, not coming out to eat or make any contact with us. This could go on for the whole length of a visit of days. No one remarked on the odd behaviour, but it spoke volumes of a dysfunctional household.

Chapter 13
First Marriage

So many things went wrong, she had to distance herself into comedy, to absolve the schlimazel in her. It started with the overdressed bride almost fainting under the canopy in an overheated synagogue; a gloomy omen, she was sure. She had asked her mum to ring the synagogue and request cutting down on the heating, but they did the opposite. The rabbi insisted on persevering with his extended sermon on "The fruit of the fruit," even though she begged him to stop, feeling about to swoon and calling for a chair to sit down.

Continuing with the bride's mother swooning at the sight of non-kosher turbot being served at the wedding repast (halibut had been ordered but the manager thought he was doing a favour upgrading it). The fact is, three turbots are not kosher—only one is—and to this day, they will never know if the rabbinical supervisor knew his onions well enough to differentiate. On every table, there was a discussion, Martin's brother was a zoologist; he didn't know. Other rabbis pointed to the shomer, the guy supervising in the kitchen.

The evening was capped in the hotel bedroom when the bride had an unexpected menstrual visitor. Apparently, her grandmother and numerous brides the world over had found themselves in the same predicament. "The last stand of virginity."

The honeymoon, apart from the groom being so bored with his beloved in the Swiss mountains that he insisted on moving down to exciting Lucerne; despite the groom being too frugal to pay for museums and opera in Venice, leaving them trudging round rain-soaked streets; despite sudden intimidating bellowing crossing a street in Strasbourg, when he said "Right" and she said "Left" the honeymoon was tolerable. A painful bout of knives from honeymoon cystitis did not add to the jollity of the trip, though.

She was welcomed back by her old friend, Margaret, "Did you cry on your honeymoon? Everyone does."

The couple settled back into their routines, staying in the flat in Highgate. The new wife naively took the advice in *Cosmopolitan*, recommending a division of labour in the kitchen from the outset. So, she suggested that Martin make supper twice a week, the worst thing she could have done, as it set the scene for domestic strife. Martin returned late on his "nights" and she sat hungry, waiting for him to start dinner. Of course, she gave up on the project, "her stomach above all." The glad news that she was pregnant lightened the atmosphere, but she worried that the Septrin antibiotic she had taken for the cystitis may have damaged the foetus. She carried on working at Central Middlesex Hospital as senior registrar in Geriatric medicine until eight weeks before delivery when maternity leave began.

Her mother and stepfather made a visit from Manchester. Martin, the husband, was abroad at a conference. Rex stormed into the flat, saying, "When are you moving to your new house? We want our flat back." Her stepfather had not realized it took time to arrange a mortgage for the townhouse they had bought in Ealing. The deposit, paid from selling the Southport house, her grandmother had given her.

She was visibly expecting by then; this enraged the jealous Rex. Distressed, she left the flat to visit friends, returning at night to find her mother had emptied all the clothes from the wardrobe onto the spare room bed. As owner, she obviously felt the right to sleep in the master bedroom.

Shocked by the big, jumbled pile of clothes on the cold, unmade bed, she sensed her life was again in turmoil (albeit in a teacup). They slept on peacefully, as she had to move the heavy mass and make up the bed, with a corresponding heavy heart and heavy load of the baby.

The husband's shouting grew in volume and frequency over petty things, such as who should remove the rubbish, and she found herself escaping by walking down the avenue, crying, the baby inside kicking in reaction.

Chapter 14
Ealing

Ethel and Martin moved to their brand-new house in Ealing, a townhouse on three floors. The galley kitchen, seven feet wide, had a gas boiler at the end under the window. She had taken maternity leave and was disturbed to come down each morning to a kitchen smelling of gas, a stuffy carbon monoxide acid odour.

She became increasingly anxious knowing the repercussions, such as Parkinson's disease, and worried about the baby. Martin thought she was mad. Eventually, she plucked up courage and called a central heating, lovely guy who built a little house for the boiler in the garden and the morning fumes disappeared.

Twenty years later, she felt vindicated when a neighbour had to have a heart-lung transplant for pulmonary hypertension. Who knows, that gas boiler may have been a causal factor?

Her life was turning out to be a soap opera or even worse, a Henry James novel. Martin's insidious meanness was raising its ugly head. Buying her first maternity clothes or plants for the garden, he would say "your cheque book" when they reached the checkout. There had been a faceoff at the

Hampstead Heath Easter fair back in High Sheldon, when she had realised his nil contribution to domestic finances. He offered twenty pounds a week.

The first rates bill arrived; it was six hundred pounds. She couldn't pay it on her senior registrar salary and turned to her mother to pay.

They took a trip to Wales to visit Martin's GP brother. A happy day, she thought, spent walking in the autumnal Wye valley followed by dinner in a country hotel. That night in bed, Martin suddenly struck her on the pregnant uterus. "Didn't he care about the baby?" her first shocked reaction. She turned over and tried to sleep, not knowing what had caused this, too shamed to ask. She supposed that she coped passively, as she assumed that she had annoyed him blithely all day, just being herself, without realising it, and he had lashed out in frustration. Maybe antipathy to marital duty caused it. Social studies reveal a third of pregnant women receive similar blows.

Next day, while buying peaches for the journey, she thought, *This marriage is not going to last*.

They never discussed the episode. It was not worth confronting him, she had learnt, as it resulted in a whirlpool of illogical anger, getting nowhere. Once, with a baby in her arms, she had requested something. Behind the closed door of his study, he yelled, "No."

"Why?" she asked pathetically. "Say please!" he roared.

In fact, an imperative does not require a please.

Now, older and wiser, with a newly labelled diagnosis to help, she can understand his fear of losing control. "Pathological Demand Avoidance" explains a lot of his Bolshie behaviour.

New Year's Day found them strolling in Beaconsfield. She still has the photo in a green maternity coat, the day before baby was born. Walking to the labour ward to be induced at Hammersmith Hospital, Martin suddenly asked her, "Where is the mortuary?" He didn't want to have to ask the way if needed.

The birth was a happy affair. She had an epidural anaesthetic; Martin stayed with her, reading the paper, and she was overjoyed to see her dark-haired beautiful daughter emerge and put into her arms.

Later, she must have had an auditory hallucination when she heard her father and sister talking in the corridor waiting to visit. No one was there—drugs or wishful thinking.

The post-natal period was hard. How do the modern mothers go home after six hours today? After a week's inpatient care, she still couldn't sit without her episiotomy rubber ring. Breastfeeding was not so encouraged then; so that the nurses and mothers could sleep at night, the babies were given complement. This did not expedite successful lactation as the babies were not so hungry and wouldn't latch on properly.

To add to the woes, she was convinced that her blood loss was excessive; her mother and the nurses poopooed it. However, she was rushed back to hospital after three months of back pain and bleeding to have an emergency op. for retained placenta, thus vindicated. Meanwhile, Martin was calling her an inadequate mother.

Mother had financed a Truby King New Zealand nanny and they spent lovely afternoons with the laughing baby, lying together on a mat playing with her. Eleanor was a smiley, curly-haired baby with big brown eyes framed by long eyelashes, a dominant gene from her grandfather.

At 33, so they decided to go for another baby, and she soon found herself pregnant again. Her medical knowledge saved this pregnancy. Yom Kippur night, she awoke to a heavy, painless haemorrhage; Martin called an ambulance.

At Hammersmith, the SHO on call wanted to abort her with a Pitocin drip but she demurred. "It could be placenta praevia."

He replied, "You are twenty-seven weeks, not the threshold twenty-eight weeks."

She persisted. "I am a doctor. Mr G treats me like a private patient—please phone him!"

He returned from the call saying, "Pethidine and the ward." The next day, the scan confirmed a placenta praevia; i.e., the placenta lying across the mouth of the womb.

A hospital bed for the next ten weeks; that SHO looked the other way whenever he passed. Another told her, "You can snuff it any time. They have ten pints of blood cross-matched for you." Martin brought Eleanor in her red suit to see her; it was a wrench. But she'd put her up in the air to see her joyous laugh. He came every day to see her. The weeks rolled by. She knitted Martin an intricate pullover in blue and white; fish and chips on a Friday. Martin's brother lent her a colour TV, new then, and she enjoyed watching *Jennie*, a serial on Churchill's mother. She was used to hospitals.

One morning, her mother woke up and said, "I feel I must visit Ethel today." She travelled alone, something she never usually did, had a quick snack in Euston station, and hurried to Ethel's room to find her being wheeled out to theatre for an emergency Caesarean section. It was dramatic; the staff had to run her to theatre with an intravenous drip going. It was the reason she had been kept in hospital all this time, in case of such an eventuality. The emeritus professor did not believe the ultrasound report and made a vertical incision right through the vascular placenta instead of a horizontal one. They had to pump blood quickly to counteract the massive bleeding. She even woke up during the anaesthetic and thought, *I know this can happen and it's happening to me*, and then went off again; the anaesthetic is kept very light to protect the baby. She had a dream or sensation that she was floating above, watching herself. In fact, she was extremely ill, a central venous line inserted into her neck to check the pressure.

The paediatrician came the next morning. She assumed the worst. "She's dead."

"She's healthier than you. She had to have a blood transfusion and is in an incubator." Born at thirty-two weeks, she weighed two kilos.

After a week, Ethel was allowed to see the baby in the neonatal ward, miles away from the postnatal ward, bad for bonding. There she lay, so vulnerable with her tubes. She looked fair with a broad forehead.

She went home without Penelope. The first night back in her own bed, she turned to Martin for a hug. No, he suddenly got angry and kicked her out of bed. Numb, she crawled back. She must have annoyed him, by turning down an invite to lunch the next day on the other side of London, not feeling up to it. Still, what a welcome home after all that.

Chapter 15
Domestic Unease

A second emergency rush to hospital for retained placenta, blood dripping down her legs. This should not happen after a Caesarean section because the surgeon has visible access to the open womb. Very soon after, another positive pregnancy test caused her alarm. She went into the garden to tell Martin, hoping for some sympathy, but his reaction was a terse, “Your problem.” A classic brush-off. She phoned her friendly obstetrician, chairman of SPUC, Society for Protection of Unborn Child. Concerned, he said, “You can’t cope. You will have to come into hospital for an abortion.” Heart-searching was obviated by a spontaneous miscarriage one quiet day. She wondered if it had been a boy.

HM69/60 was a scheme for child-bearing women to stay in the rat race and work part-time. It was a blessing, career-wise, and she stayed on it for six years as a part-time senior registrar.

By now, she had an Australian day nanny who went home when she returned from work. Penelope, her new daughter, was beautiful with the long limbs and body of her family going back to her grandmother. She was so fastidious she wouldn’t feed unless her nappy was changed. Ethel’s father, a good doctor, on a visit noticed that the baby had gaze aversion and mentioned a diagnosis.

She managed to juggle the different tasks by going to bed early; Martin was a night owl. Even after a late-night partying, he would come up an hour after her, saying, "I have to unwind." She took to wearing earplugs so as not to be disturbed and was forced to write him a sad letter begging him to come to bed with her once a month. He refused.

Coming home after a meeting in the hospital, she heard Eleanor screaming. Martin said, "Eleanor has been crying all evening with earache. There's nothing wrong with her." She hurried upstairs to find her standing in her cot, red-faced and howling. She lifted her out, comforted her, then examined her ears with an auroscope. Her eardrum was bright red with bubbles, something she had never seen in all her two years doing ENT. She gave her some analgesic and antibiotic and stayed till she fell asleep.

They rented a cottage in Cornwall for a week. Eleanor developed a fever; Martin took off for the day with Penelope, saying, "I'm not staying in on my week of holiday." She felt downcast and abandoned and rang her mum for some comfort. Another example of Martin's lack of empathy, which took forty years to be explained, as a probable Asperger's Syndrome.

Escalation of the verbal and physical abuse began to dominate life. Bellowing, when the air seemed to move, in response to peccadilloes was frequent and unsettling. Once, the nanny and she hid behind a wardrobe, they were so scared of him; commenting, "When G-d made Martin, he threw away the mould." Another time, he twisted her arm in the kitchen in a half Nelson after she questioned why he wouldn't wear the polo neck sweater she had bought him.

On the motorway to Manchester, Martin lost his temper, pulled her hair, and bent her arm whilst driving. In a traffic jam, she escaped to seek refuge in the car behind. The driver let her in, saying, "I have been watching your husband hitting you." He told her he lived in Chester and that his wife had multiple sclerosis. At the next service station, she searched the car park for the family car and returned to a peaceful onward journey to Manchester.

Walking into her mother's beautiful orange, blue, and white kitchen in Prestwich, her daughter announced, "Daddy tried to break Mummy's arm."

The Queen's Silver Jubilee, a gala fireworks display on the South Bank, was planned. She was looking forward to it. Leaving Ealing, her husband noticed they were low on fuel. "If we run out of petrol, you can walk to the nearest petrol station and I'll go home by tube."

"Let's go home then," she said. He turned around. Back alone in her bedroom, she looked out of the window onto the dark garden, forlorn and disappointed.

Martin was awarded a three-month Royal Society fellowship at the Technion in Haifa. He accepted and went on ahead. She followed three weeks later with the two little ones and their paraphernalia; her parents came down to help her at the airport. She settled into the flat at the top of Mount Carmel in Kiryat Hatechnion, a staff complex.

A harsh time ensued there, hauling prams up flights of stairs, washing nappies and clothes in the bath, but she didn't complain. However, Martin's easily triggered roaring got her down.

Once, she noticed a wet patch on his pyjamas. "Are you wanking?" she asked him.

"Yes, I've done it every night since I was young," he answered. "That is your competition." She was flabbergasted after three years of marriage to discover this fact. There is an Israeli saying, "To know someone, you have to eat a sack of salt with them." It sure takes a long time to figure people out.

We paid a visit to her cousins, in Jerusalem; they lived in a lovely house by now in Givat Hamivtar. Rotem said he would sound out the situation and took Martin for a long walk on Shabbat. He returned, looking white, needing two glasses of water. "You will have to get a divorce," he warned. "Martin has just given me a list as long as my arm of complaints against you." Much later, she learnt that Rotem had also given her husband the advice to be tough with her and that partly explained his subsequent behaviour.

The crisis came soon after.

Getting off the bus with the pram holding the two girls, she swung a bag of shopping containing a purse full of coppers somehow against her calf. She sustained a painful haematoma in the muscle; she could hardly walk. She limped back to the flat, got the children playing and rested with a wet tea towel wrapped around as a compress, and waited for Martin to come home for lunch.

No concern! Just abuse yelled for not washing up the breakfast things plus accusations of malingering. He ate his lunch and stormed back to his office, leaving her feeling desolate. She was a doctor after all; she knew how to make a simple diagnosis.

At sunset, she fed the children and put them to bed. Feeling very low, she wrote a note to Martin telling him she had taken three Mogadon sleeping tablets at his unjust treatment. He kept this note and used it in the divorce, as evidence that she was not fit to look after her daughters.

She took the Mogadon and went to sleep; she knew one could not kill oneself with an overdose of these tablets but just needed to get out of this unbearable situation for a while.

Martin returned, read the note, and left her sleeping till morning. He made no attempt to wake her or get help for her. The next day, he did insist she go alone to the hospital, still unbelieving that she had a genuine injury to her calf muscle.

Of course, they corroborated her diagnosis, and prescribed rest and a compression bandage. It would resolve itself. He perused the report and became a little kinder. A week later, she was allowed to take a trip north to the Golan while he looked after the girls.

There were some good moments. Penelope on her second birthday, walked for the first time to get a sweet from the lady at the cash desk in the cafeteria. Marietta, her old medic friend, now living in Haifa, married with three children, had a chocolate mousse party for Eleanor's third birthday. Visits to Martin's brother and family in the kibbutz; Martin's professor took them out to the beach, though it was cold on that January day, before they left. Then, back to Ealing to the final chapter of this marriage.

She would go to work crying; a lovely social worker, Mrs Bevan, finally said to her, this can't go on, you must split. Once, so frustrated, she even took a pair of scissors and cut up the pullover she had knitted him in hospital. One night, when she was putting three-year-old Eleanor to bed, she said, "I want Daddy to live in Leeds or Liverpool or across the road in Zara's house." Always a wise child, this decided her; she was only staying for the children.

In desperation, not knowing what to do next, she looked up the name of a probation officer in a small office in Ealing. He listened quietly to her. "You must put the children in the car and drive to Manchester straight away," which she did. Relieved, she went home, packed, and calmly left the house with the girls. The drive up the motorway was long and snarled up, but she had escaped.

Chapter 16
The First Divorce

She sat on the sofa with Martin. "I think we should get a divorce," she said quietly. "We have had a year of marriage guidance counselling, which only resulted in us quarrelling all the way home in the car." She had also consulted a psychiatrist who specialised in marital problems, whose only comment had been, "His choice of work in mathematics reveals his character, not easy." Martin nodded. "But only on condition you petition me first then I cross-petition you."

"That means the High Court, a lot of expense and hassle, and in the end, we will get a divorce. Why not do it simply and by agreement?"

"No." He had obviously thought this through and was adamant.

Papworth, her membership tutor, had done a survey, confirming that everyone seeking help from marriage guidance counsellors ended up getting divorced. It's clear that professional psychiatric advice is the only way of untangling the interactions of two troubled aspirants, not amateur do-gooders. Too late for us.

So, on her first visit to the kindly white-haired solicitor in Wembley, it was explained that she had to give a full account in her petition, as once submitted to the High Court of Justice, no allegation could be added. She had to go home and write a full essay of her life with Martin, the bad bits only.

She was instructed to stop washing, cooking, and sleeping with her husband as a sign that the marriage had broken down irretrievably. They had their last coming together, then she moved into a different bedroom. It was strangely cold-blooded and sad at the same time.

Her big worry was how her girls were taking it all. The child psychiatrist agreed to talk to her at Hammersmith Hospital; the best advice he could give her was to tell them that they both still loved them very much and that it was not their fault. It was helpful.

Things progressed but Martin showed no sign of moving out. Got worse, in fact, bellowing over washing in the garage, throwing the contents of the full basket over the car, parked there. She managed to let her stepfather hear the roaring over the phone and this convinced him of the seriousness of the problem. She dreamt that her husband fell off the stool in the kitchen, keeling over with a heart attack. Felt bad about it but that's wishful thinking—the subconscious took over.

Eventually, in despair, she consulted the local probation officer, because a social worker was unavailable, and took his advice to flee to Manchester.

Once settled in her old bedroom, the girls in their cots, they began the business of an injunction to get Martin out of the house. Her stepfather, who had barely looked her in the eye to say two words all through the marriage, couldn't do enough to help her now. They tried to claim legal aid, to no avail.

She bought legal paper from Oyez, the lawyers' stationery shop, and they set about preparing the affidavits for the local family solicitor, who took over the case.

The refrain, "If a snake could bake a cake, what kind of cake would a snake bake?" characterised that period. They were more relaxed in the Mancunian sunshine, the lovely garden, and local playgrounds, with Grandma around enjoying their company.

Hard work ensued, getting four affidavits, the first from her next-door neighbour in Ealing. He was quite willing to reveal that on more than one occasion, he had stood outside the front door debating with the opposite neighbour whether to intervene at Martin's roaring; being English, they decided not to.

Not so the Israeli neighbour in Haifa, Professor L, who knocked at the door to tell her that her husband was not a decent human being, and it was bad for the children. He sent her the affidavit. Years later, as president of the Technion, she met his wife, who said she always wondered "why you did not shout back."

She found the gardener, who had witnessed through the French windows Eleanor spilling coffee down her chest, to defend herself from the claim in Martin's counter-petition that she had deliberately poured the hot liquid over her daughter. She had rushed her to Hammersmith Hospital for treatment of the scald. Martin had brought chocolates home that afternoon. The last affidavit was painstaking, but she traced the man who gave her a lift on the motorway. He had told her he lived in Chester and that his wife had multiple sclerosis. The multiple sclerosis society was the key, and he happily gave her the sworn statement needed.

We obtained the injunction and Martin moved out to university accommodation. There was a tragic postscript in that Martin's father had a sudden heart attack and died shortly after. She suspected there was a link with the disgrace involved; he was a decent character, and she was sorry.

She offered to do some surgeries for Rex, to pay her way a little, whilst staying with them in Manchester. One evening, after doing one, Rex was in a euphoric mood, opening a bottle of wine, strangely jolly. That night, Eleanor told her, as she put her to bed, "Rex said in his study, if I say I am in love with you, will you say you are in love with me?" Eleanor had astutely noted that something was not quite right and that there was a difference between "I love you" and "I am in love with you." The chickens had come home to roost, and that long shadow made Ethel determined not to leave the girls alone with Rex again.

On the train, travelling back to London to attend the court with her mother, she read Martin's cross-petition. It was so ludicrous; they were laughing out loud as she quoted the funny bits. He put, "Her mother changed her vest four times a day; and that his wife wore a vest in bed; that she used to like Moshe Dayan and now she doesn't; that she only read items in the newspaper about medicine and Israel; that her stepfather gets the cleaner to check the Financial Times index every afternoon on the TV." If these were the worst claims he could find?

She now had a barrister, a strict man with clipped speech, and together, with her solicitor, they entered the High Court in the Strand. Statues of Solomon and Moses flanked the impressive pseudo-gothic building, but a stone cat and dog, representing fighting litigants, humoured the nerves. They waited on a bench in a long corridor to be called into the carved oak-lined court. They went on to win two high court cases. Martin, a litigant in person, had claimed custody of the children and maintenance from her.

Anxious about having an anti-Semitic judge, he was in fact Jewish, and when M insisted on being called doctor, saying he was a PhD and she was only a Bachelor of Medicine, Judge Balfour said to him, "Sit down, Doctor!"

The most beautiful finale was the ceremony of the "get," the Jewish divorce. She enjoyed it more than the wedding, it was so interesting. The husband gives his wife the get and the grounds are usually "no shalom bayit," peace in the house.

We entered the Court of the Beth Din near Woburn Square to find three dayanim (judges) sitting up on the bench; a scribe was ready nearby.

Establishment of names came first. The dayans were shocked that she and her sister were both named Mia; her father had forgotten her at that crucial naming. It was an exquisitely important fact, or Martin could have been said to have divorced her sister instead of her—no joke.

Her father's name was queried as an unknown name.

They even brought an encyclopaedia to check it all out.

The scribe chanted her name Ethel Mia, daughter of N, each time he read it out, to distinguish from her sister, Mia, daughter of G.

Eventually, they had to leave while the scribe wrote the manuscript on parchment. When they trooped back after a coffee break, Martin had to swear that he had not been coerced into signing in the interim.

The ceremony ended when she held out her cupped hands, into which Martin dropped the Bill of Divorcement and the dayan told her she was free to marry anyone except a cohen (priest) after three months.

She then backed slowly out of the court.

Compared to the sullying details of the civil divorce, this was freeing. It was an all-good pure feeling and made her proud of being Jewish.

That "free to marry" took an abyss of thirty-five years. Now a single parent, and working part-time as senior registrar at Charing Cross Hospital, she settled into her new life.

Jumping for joy in their narrow hall, when Eleanor, aged four, passed her first test for the Prep. of the local high school by describing what she saw through the headmistress's window. She had to draw a picture of herself and left out the arms. So did her sister in her drawings; Ethel was alarmed to realise this must mean loss of her dad. However, Eleanor did put a large shining sun in the corner, which apparently is an important sign of well-being. Mother offered to pay the school fees.

Martin became the perfect ex-husband; he had found the right amount of distance and commitment, was reliable on access plans, and was helpful in emergencies. A leaking pipe whilst she was stuck at a committee meeting brought him promptly to sort it out. On another occasion, she was struck with migraine, and he came to take the girls.

She managed by going to bed shortly after they did. Up at seven, as she was an early riser. She had a condition called Advanced Sleep Progression, a genetic tendency to sleep early and wake early, a "lark" in common parlance. Sunset was enough to enable sleep.

Mother's helps were vital and they went through some characters, a Russian, Mrs Boboschka who made piroshky

Eleanor hated her so that was that. Then a plump Brazilian, who made spinach patties and accused Ethel of assault when she patted her on the arm, so that was that.

We fixed on a beautiful, calm Swedish girl, Helena, who struck up with a pilot. He used to creep in directly from his flights and was gone in the morning. They never saw him, but she eventually married him and took him back to Sweden. She sent pictures of her babies.

Helena had been perceptive in telling her in conversation that she tended to look at Eleanor more than Penelope, discussed at our breakfast bar in the tiny, cramped galley kitchen. Aeons later, she stood accused of a similar crime, looking at her grandson more than her granddaughters. The routine became dropping the girls off at school across the road, then driving through the traffic where Hammersmith roundabout, the worst in Europe, had to be negotiated, three times a week, en route to Charing Cross Hospital in Fulham Palace Road.

Her boss was Dr C, a charming, very English man who had been stabbed by an anti-vivisectionist and lost his spleen. The new high-rise building was pleasant to work in, but they had to be careful what they said in lifts during their peripatetic ward rounds.

A first long-haul flight to Brazil with friends was a jolly interlude, while the children were holidaying with their father. Rio and Copacabana Beach were exotic enough, "The Girl from Ipanema" sung by a long-mourned lost suitor, followed her down the wide, beautifully paved promenade.

Life was peaceful. As the Italians say, "Melio Solo Che Mal Accompagnato."

Chapter 17
A Great Love

Israel was back in the news. Arafat and his Fatah brigade were expelled from Jordan during Black September 1970; they entered Lebanon and fomented violence in Israel. A bus hijack on the coastal road led to a shootout, where thirty-eight Israelis, including thirteen children, were killed and seventy-six wounded. This massacre caused Israel to invade Lebanon three days later in 1978 and pushed the Palestinian Liberation Organisation north to the Litani River.

The PLO colonised Southern Lebanon. It was a state within a state, as they used it as a base for raids on civilian targets in Israel, as well as worldwide terror attacks.

Israel had to invade again in 1982 and forcibly expelled the PLO to Tunis with house-to-house fighting, as far as Beirut. Israel later withdrew from Lebanon, keeping control of a twelve-mile security buffer zone, policed by United Nations Forces. Despite this ongoing strife, they were invited to join her parents in the summer of 1980 in Netanya. She picked the girls up after school at midday and caught the afternoon El Al flight.

By evening, they had arrived in the hotel, unpacked, and gone down to the lobby to greet her mother and Rex. Sitting with them was a white-haired, tanned man with a weathered face. Ethel complained to her mother afterwards that he had cheek to stare at her so blatantly in an effort to score.

This was Mischa Richman, a new Russian friend of Rex, who was to be a strong influence in her life.

That first night in the hotel, there was a wedding. The bride, still in her white dress, jumped into the floodlit pool very late to the cheers of everyone. They leaned over their bedroom balconies, watching the joie de vivre, and went to sleep happy to be in Israel.

Mischa had an easy sophistication, speaking Russian to Rex and then switching to English when turning to her mother. He knew intuitively to concentrate on her only when Rex was not around, then they talked in simple Hebrew. A powerful man, who had left his family in Tashkent in 1934 to be a pioneer in Palestine, he never saw his parents again. A farmer, he'd given his elder son his avocado and pepper farm, situated around Tabba on Lake Galilee, where the miracle of the loaves and fishes took place, commemorated by a monastery with wonderful mosaics. They later attended a concert in the courtyard, one magical summer's evening.

Now divorced, he was teaching his younger son, Oded, the hotelier, the ropes as he himself managed the hotel, Gan Hashoshanim as part owner. There was a big age difference. He was the same age as her mother, born in 1915; she was forty-one. She did not know this at the time.

Meanwhile, Rex had decided to buy the flat in the twin block, adjacent to Mischa on the fourth floor. Indeed, one could look straight through into his kitchen window and beyond from Ethel's kitchen. Within a week, they had completed the conveyance, bought the furniture in a kibbutz factory, and moved in, Rex saying, "I am not paying for a hotel when I have a flat." Mischa noticed that she was given the cheapest and grottiest furniture for her bedroom with sadness and later mentioned it to his friend. They hastily got her an upgrade.

Rex was showing a bit too much physical attention to Penelope, sitting her on his knee and stroking her affectionately; Ethel took note with foreboding. She had instructed her mum to stay with them when she wasn't there and was angry to learn later that Mother had gone to her bedroom and left them alone in his clutches. She never let them go to stay in Manchester by themselves.

In time, her mother added soft furnishings and Rex imported huge chandeliers as they reminded him of Poland. There was no balcony, the fashion then, as people were only closing them in to make an additional room.

A postage stamp of sea through the high-rise blocks was still visible; the decision was taken not to buy a sea prospect as terrorists were landing in boats, taking hostages. It happened in Maalot, where a horrific massacre of twenty-five schoolchildren took place, after a two-day hostage taking of a hundred people in a booby-trapped school; sixty-nine were wounded. A new steel security door was invented called Rav Bariach at that time; they had bolts extending horizontally and vertically into the lintel. Naval boats and helicopters now patrol the coastline constantly. Each new terrorist threat produces its ingenious and vital response.

The first inkling was her looking out for Mischa's blue car as she came and went to the beach with the girls, now aged six and seven, or watching for his white-headed figure to appear at the hotel pool gates.

She therefore gave a willing "Yes" to his dinner invite, up dark steps to a bistro off Stampa Street.

It was exciting to be with someone who attracted her, after the dates with deadly defensive types. He quickly understood her inhibitions and innate shyness with men, which returned, despite having been a married woman.

The arch seducer, that she later learned he was, he knew to make no physical approach until she must have shown how much she had wanted it.

The point came after a revealing and crazy drive round the sleazy nightclubs of Netanya to obtain those elusive packages, which she insisted on. It was an initiation into true pleasure.

Disbelief exists as to the possibility, but his "Elgar cello concerto" slowly trained her to mutual orgasm by saying "bo, nigmor b'yachad (come, let's finish together)" as the trigger. He had told her that on his bar mitzvah, he had taken down a girl's knickers in the barn and had his first sexual experience. From that time, he had never "used his hand," as he put it. She decided this explained why he was such a good lover; learning the right way from the start.

The unwitting parents went home, and they followed later; Mischa took them to the airport. She returned to Charing Cross and began counting the days till his promised trip to her in London.

She took the girls to see *Annie* in Shepherd's Bush and the song lyrics "Tomorrow, tomorrow, I love you, tomorrow, it's only a day away" became a symbol of her longing.

After months of waiting, she was driving to Gatwick excitedly to pick him up. Seeing his solid figure emerge so befuddled her that they got lost on the way back. Toys for the children, who had gone to stay with Martin, and a pendant watch for her set the happy tone.

Together to the candlelit synagogue for Kol Nidre, the night of Yom Kippur. Later, on the blue carpet in the lounge, she could not refuse him, although it was forbidden on such a night.

Trips to Cambridge, the Tower of London, and *Evita* followed when the refrain "Don't cry for me, Argentina" reflected her anguish at his imminent departure.

Rex caught wind of his visit and, suspicious, came flying down from Manchester to take him to stay in their Highgate flat. The last she saw of Mischa on that trip was at a chamber concert of Dvorak's Quintet at the Queen Elizabeth Hall. She sat separately with her mother, feigning a cool acquaintance with Mischa. Back in Israel, he requested the record, which she sent off.

The pattern was set; work, the girls, and stolen visits to Netanya. Soon her detective powers realised that this man, surrounded by bathing beauties at his hotel, could not resist the temptations of those girls, hungry for a holiday romance. A warning from his daughter-in-law of how much his wife had suffered plus postcards from lovelorn Swedes did not deter her, despite the pain. She brought the girls each summer. They loved him too, a kind of grandfather. They would walk along the rosemary-fragrant cliff top to Gan Hashoshanim for a Friday night dinner, a big treat.

He did come to London for a second visit, but it was marred by his making a play for her au pair, who resisted him, saying, "She has been waiting for you to come so long." She drove him to Norwich and the coast, staying in B&Bs, and sailed to visit the seals. This time "Memory," from a visit to *Cats*, made him buy that record,

He did love her in his way. On one of her visits to Israel, he returned from buying his burial plot in Tel Aviv with a beautiful five-diamond ring, probably to cheer himself up too. She loved it, but soon lost it down the toilet at the hotel, still the schlemiel. The insurance gave her a new modern one, which she still wears.

In 1982, a turning point occurred; she was unemployed, doing some gardening, when the phone rang. It was Giselle, an old medical friend, asking her to apply for the post of consultant geriatrician. Thrilled, she prepared with an interview specialist in Croydon and bought a black suit from Jaeger. Bruno O'Harris, a friend, rang her to say the decision was unanimous; she was appointed. Now she was trapped in England and remembered Mischa saying, "Tgadli et hayeladim (Go bring up the children)!" He had no intention of leaving his beloved Israel.

This was a full-time post, shared with a brilliant colleague. Giselle Said had studied medicine in Agra, India and was able to go from bed to bed speaking Gujarati, Punjabi, and umpteen other languages—Polish, Finnish, Hungarian, whatever was necessary. Ethel settled into the job slowly, her innate inferiority complex battling with the big bluff she had to present to the world. A large, jolly Sri Lankan registrar intuited when she needed support. She adored him but he disappeared when Saddam Hussein invaded Kuwait as he got stuck there.

Eleanor was a problem, having recurrent tonsil infections, and her persistent cough, heard at night, was knives in Ethel's heart. A consultant paediatric ENT surgeon at Westminster refused to remove them. Coming triumphantly out of theatre, he proclaimed "I only took out her adenoids" to her sinking heart. Two more years of tonsillitis with antibiotics ensued, till a Hammersmith hospital ENT surgeon obliged; she was vindicated as Eleanor never looked back afterwards. Each episode of surgery is a trauma for the mother, waiting outside the theatre for her daughter to emerge safe and sound.

In 1985, Mischa invited her over for a weekend, saying he had something to ask her, so after work on a Thursday she flew to stay in his flat. He asked her to marry him. However, when he went off to work the next morning, she opened the fridge.

There, was a package wrapped in a German newspaper, dated two days before, a stinking salted herring nestled inside. The ghastly realisation that he had had a German visitor the day before swamped her into sobs. Half a bottle of his vodka later, he came home in time to hold her head over the toilet bowl.

That was the end of serious thoughts of marriage. She just couldn't bring two little ones out of their country to live with such a fickle man.

In other ways, Mischa had a very good influence on her by suggesting that she have therapy; he also talked seriously to her about finances, showing her how the parents should help her.

She would arrive back in UK and telephone him to find a woman answering; it was not the cleaner. All this altered her behaviour at work and with the girls, making her bad-tempered.

The next time she visited Netanya, Mischa had a woman living blatantly with him, as evidenced by the images in his kitchen. She had to lump it.

She always loved him and was happy to run after him in the street if she spied his figure on subsequent visits.

Chapter 18
A Domestic Transformation

Her elder daughter, Eleanor, loved going to stay with her Aunt Mia in Manchester. The warm house filled with biennial new babies (ten altogether), visitors, neighbours popping in, and a generally chaotic atmosphere, until it came to the time for Shabbat and festivals.

The day before, cooking began in earnest; Friday, the table set for about twelve, including guests, baths, best clothes, candle lighting at sunset, and a festive atmosphere.

There were strictures, of course, no radio, television, putting on lights, which were on a time switch anyway. The women sat and waited for Josh, brother-in-law, to return from synagogue with his boys. Hungry, they stood around the table for Kiddush, the blessing over wine, then the washing of hands and no talking until after the prayer for bread. A four-course meal of gefilte fish with potato salad, red beetroot chraine and loads of other salads, followed by chicken soup with matzo balls. A main course of chicken with potato kugel and vegetables and a heavy dessert such as crumble. The reason for her brother-in-law's increasing girth was due to huge proportions, and the inevitable diabetes began in late middle age.

The following day, another meal round the table with discussions on the weekly portion of the law or children's squabbles adding to the family atmosphere.

So, when Eleanor was eleven, she asked her whether they could become orthodox too, believing it gave them the best chance of being a happy family she wanted to follow their example. A little sad, but Ethel agreed readily as she had always had a leaning towards being religious, but her stepfather had brainwashed her out of it, as an atheistic survivor of the Holocaust.

She turned to Rabbi Morris, may his memory be blessed, her lovely mentor. Rabbi Morris first appeared in their house in Ealing, at the behest of her sister, who asked him to check the mezuzoth, the little boxes you see nailed to the right-hand side of Jewish doorposts. The prayer "The Shema" is handwritten on rolled parchment inside. Some joke, it says, "Help! Help! I am a prisoner in a mezuzah factory."

Actually, it affirms the oneness of the Almighty. Damage to them in any way is surmised to bring family problems, so they must be checked regularly. This smiling, bearded man changed all their spoiled mezuzahs, went home, and said to his wife, "Today I met a wonderful woman." Subsequently, they became as close as family, visiting each other often.

One exciting day, Rabbi M with another Lubavitcher arrived with blowlamps, cauldrons, and cameras to make the house strictly kosher. The kitchen was turned upside down, all utensils plunged into the boiling vat of water. The oven and hob seared clean with the blowlamp. It took a full day. Even the dishwasher did not escape.

She was a bit humiliated, but also proud to be featured in their monthly magazine with photographs of the procedure.

Ethel's transformation to a modern orthodox woman (a category in itself) was completed by giving her a "chrevuta." A voluntary friendly teacher, a glamorous interior designer, dedicated a weekly lesson to her on the niceties of becoming "Shomer Shabbat"—that is, keeping the Shabbat—as strictly as her sister Mia did. It was a gentle process, not being expected to change radically overnight, and could be taken at its own pace. It was difficult, the long summer Saturday evening with no radio to keep her company, having to wait until sunset when Shabbat went out and secular activities could be resumed.

It was worth it in the end. A more peaceful lifestyle. No tramping down Oxford Street with the two girls, fighting for a dressing room in crowded shops, coming home exhausted, after a week working in the hospital. Transport was also forbidden on the Sabbath, so they walked everywhere.

Transformation accomplished! It took over a year. Writing in soft wax is quick and easy. Similarly, it is erased quickly and easily. To engrave in stone is slow and painstaking but irremovable and long-lasting.

Chapter 19
Oh to Be a Consultant in the NHS

By the 1980s, women were well established as hospital doctors, especially in the junior ranks, and she never encountered prejudice as she progressed up the ladder. However, the male dominance remained at consultant level and many women consultants had a very hard time maintaining their position. She found that she was no exception.

She had a wonderful post at a West London hospital, the girls were at a very good school across the road, and the situation was ideal; if they needed her, she was a drive away by car.

She'd just finished the three-hour multidisciplinary ward round, ending with tea and biscuits in the sister's office. It had been lively, the physio, O.T., social worker, and district nurse all contributing.

She loved these ward rounds, picking out the diagnoses, following patients' progress, and discussing moot points with the junior staff. They learnt from one another; it was good to encourage their flashes of brilliant observation. One young doctor diagnosed, just from viewing the back of the eye, with an ophthalmoscope, evidence of subacute bacterial endocarditis. The Roth spots, he saw, led them to take blood cultures, which grew bacteria, so they were able to treat the heart infection with antibiotics. They later presented that case at the weekly meeting of medical staff.

She went down to lunch. They sat at the consultants' table mostly airing nasty things about absent colleagues. Institutional life does include delicious gossip. Frequent piano recitals were a joy, given by the concert pianist turned diabetologist, who got them a Yamaha piano somehow. Beethoven's sonatas would set them off, invigorated for the afternoon.

False rumours spread over the years about Ethel, such as "she had fallen for an Indian houseman; she had invested in care homes." Some of her nicknames became known to her as "the Enema queen," "Mother Teresa," even "the Devil."

A strange phenomenon usually occurred on Friday mornings, when she would find a case of retention of urine. This is an inability to pass urine so the bladder fills up to the umbilicus. Drugs, constipation, being bed-bound can be the cause. If untreated, the knock-on effect is kidney failure. This invariably happens in outliers, those scattered on other wards around the hospital when their beds are full. So, beware!

She'd see a patient sitting in a chair or bed looking pregnant with a bulging lower abdomen and pounce, examining the tense football of the swollen bladder. The treatment was simple, catheterisation to drain the bladder, stop the culprit drugs, or enemas to clear the faecal impaction. Hence the nickname Enema Queen.

She returned one Monday to be told such a patient had died. Suspicious, she investigated to discover that the nurse had not catheterised, as instructed, leading to the very rare rupture of the bladder; although the patient had been calling out in pain all weekend, according to the notes. She reported it to the senior nurse in the hierarchy but heard nothing more. Maybe a sign of her weak authority; the nurse felt no compunction to carry out the order.

She probably made a dangerous enemy of the Dr X, inadvertently, by remarking that he should check his liver function; his high whisky intake was a known. Later, when she requested his second opinion on a patient she thought had TB, he forbade her, being a purist, to start treatment until the diagnosis was confirmed bacteriologically, often a fruitless task. So, the poor man had to die to prove himself a phthisis case on post-mortem. After that, she would give the patient a therapeutic trial herself, without calling him. That is, to treat with anti-tuberculous drugs and, if the patient got better, putting on weight, etc. It was proven. If not, they stopped the drugs.

Like a shark swimming around the hospital, choosing which consultant to target for the next witch hunt, Dr X ousted the competent chemical pathologist, a paediatrician, a psychiatrist, and a new young glamorous female obstetrician. This puissant doctor, now appointed medical director, preferred his sinister politics to medicine. These "successes" seemed to give him a power thrill.

Medical social workers were frustrating, as they could take weeks or months to discharge their cured patients back home. This was their job, to arrange services or care homes. They didn't seem to feel the pressure the doctors were under to find empty beds for the sick piling up in casualty. They were not alone. A famous paper was published, "Bed blocking in Bromley," wherein the appointment of a lay placement officer solved everything. Ethel seized the "cause celebre" and persuaded her faithful secretary to take on such a post. Efficiency increased enormously, causing resentment in the social work department, hence Ethel's moniker, "the Devil."

The director of social work at the town hall wrote an article stating, "Collaboration with the doctor is collaboration with the enemy." The social workers felt they were protecting the patient from the doctor; such was the ethos; some were Marxist too. She felt they weren't as professional as the physios and occupational therapists. The doctors needed the beds and appeared unfeeling to the tardy MSWs. Extant today, thirty years later, the same problems are aired on the radio and in the press as an election topic. Boris Johnson, prime minister, promised to solve the social system. They are still waiting.

It was subtle, the breakdown of her position. Initially, on the rota to give lectures which people seemed to enjoy; on occasions she could boast standing room only. Suddenly, her name just wasn't on the list.

This witch hunting was becoming widespread. Wendy Savage, the first woman consultant to be appointed in obstetrics and member of the General Medical Counsel, was accused of incompetence in 1985 by a professor in her department and suspended from the London hospital. She was cleared in a high-profile enquiry; there were public protests by women, devoted after her wonderful treatment. The *British Medical Journal* gave her the Outstanding Contribution to Health Award. Other witch hunts followed.

Late in the job, the female senior manager invited the women consultants to a meeting. She asked if they felt "disadvantaged" (nice word for persecuted) in any way. One by one, each explained how they had rationalised to themselves why this was so.

The bacteriologist thought it was because she was Arab, the rheumatologist because she was Jewish and divorced, and so on round the room. "No," the director explained, "it's because women manage differently from men. They take junior staff into their confidence in a friendly way whereas men give orders authoritatively." Truly enlightening, explaining the teasing of her friendliness with junior staff. Gender politics.

Money was behind some of this. Men feared the women would take over their private practice on "the street" as Harley was known. She was never interested in kowtowing to those paying.

Also, there was the unspoken issue of the merit awards, which were nominated by the consultants to each other, adding a huge increment to the salary and final pension. She was never so blessed as she didn't deserve it, but other women must have been.

The misogynistic tactics continued, as evidenced by a grand catered party made for a retiring surgeon; when her brilliant lady colleague retired, only the ward food trolley was rattled in.

One of the worst things ever said to her was by a new geriatrician Dr Z, really a gastroenterologist manqué. He came into her office and said, "Every consultant in this hospital wants you to leave." Then walked away. She was devastated. "It's not true," her Welsh colleague comforted her. Funny how one remembers the insults and not the compliments in life.

A moment of glory; she presented a case at the grand round in Hammersmith Hospital, then the Postgraduate Medical School (her appointment included honorary senior lecturer there).

Under the innocuous title of "Bruising in the Elderly," she described a Parkinsonian lady with suspicious bruises on her thighs. How she had drawn the curtains around the bed, sat beside her, and asked bluntly after a chat, "Has your son ever sexually abused you?"

She replied, "Boys will be boys. There's no shame that it happened." Her son was educationally subnormal.

Elder abuse was just coming into the open, so she covered all aspects; physical, mental, financial, medicinal. A kindly geriatrician told her the talk was widely acclaimed. A new blue, black Jaeger suit helped.

They particularly enjoyed our weekly sessions with the haematologist. They would gaze at the projected slides of our patients' blood films.

So much could be inferred from his expert surveillance. The red cells, their shapes and sizes revealing iron deficiency, leukaemia; the blue spots of lead poisoning were a rare excitement to behold as well as red fragments from haemolysis. They may have noticed the odd visitor of the malarial parasite in the red cell as the hospital was near an airport and would catch the odd traveler. A surfeit of platelet cells pointed to bleeding somewhere in the body, thus revealing the cause of an anaemia. They would often come away with new ideas for diagnosis and management of the patient. Whether an infection was caused by a virus or bacteria; an increase of specific cells called monocytes directed us to possible tuberculosis, glandular fever, or subacute endocarditis. It was a treasure trove to the initiated. Sadly, nowadays, the bloods are calibrated by a machine, so a special request is needed for the blood film to be examined by the haematologist.

The bed-blocking hassle increased from the medical social work department. She drove to a health farm in the country on Martin's weekend to have the children. Pre-sauna, her blood pressure was found to be sky high, 180/110, called malignant hypertension. Thus, her life was saved, dramatic but true. The job, the politics, the girls, and horrible men friends had all combined to cause this crisis. She was fifty-one years old and both parents and grandparents had suffered hypertension.

Monday, an ECG, pushed through her letterbox by the GP, revealed frightening early left ventricular strain and left bundle branch block in the heart. She took her daughter's bike and cycled around Ealing in a defiant reaction. Prof. C at Hammersmith consoled her after listening to her chest, saying, "There are no crepitations at your lung bases."

I should hope not," she thought. *That's a sign of actual heart failure.* She started treatment with beta blockers and took a week off. It soon got around the hospital. She was called to the new director in his office; he advised her to take early retirement. She had been there eleven years.

Not only at work but at home, she stumbled upon a problem, visiting Penelope's bedroom. On her desk were lists of her daily food intake including calorie counts; 900, 800, 950. All was suddenly clear, Penelope's new habit of cooking herself a big fry-up of mixed vegetables for supper.

Her drop in two bra sizes. She faced her, Penelope said eleven girls in her class were doing the same. Penelope was sixteen.

She took her to Eileen, her therapist, who was an expert in anorexia, and then to Hampstead to buy her some nice clothes. She nearly cried when she saw Penelope's winged scapulae sticking out and how very thin she was. Eileen explained that the anorexic feels or wants to be invisible, and to cure it one has to harness her obsessional side, using a dietitian, who would explain how to eat properly and nutritiously without putting on weight.

The GP referred her to a dietitian. Ethel told Penelope that she couldn't go on her planned youth trip to Israel until the dietitian discharged her. She sent Martin a letter, asking him to take her out on her own, and flatter her. A father's attention is especially important to make her feel less invisible, yet attractive.

About this time came the dreaded visit from the shark, Dr X. He bumbled into her outpatient clinic and intimated it was her time to go.

All these things pointed one way. Also, Penelope's need finally decided her. She handed in her resignation and concentrated on her daughter, making sponge cakes with six eggs as desperate recourse. Apparently, it's classical that anorexics stop eating protein, thus explaining the vegetable fry-ups.

Slowly they pulled Penelope out of it and she was able to go on the Israel tour. Phew!

On her last day, she brought a bottle of wine and cheesecake and told her team after the ward round, in the sister's office. No one knew that she was leaving. The district nurse and her secretary cried, and people were upset; the diabetic specialist gave flowers.

That afternoon, H M, an old friend, came to say goodbye in her office, whose door never had her name affixed as all the male consultants had. He told her that she had had the most letters of praise from patients. She hadn't seen a single one of them.

As she stopped at the lights on her way home, a senior nurse drew up and opened her window. "It's nothing against you; it was strategy against geriatrics," she called out to her. So it was. After she left, they disbanded the geriatric department. Dr Z became the hospital gastroenterologist and her Welsh colleague the endocrinologist.

She heard from a radiologist friend that the shark, who had helped drive her out, came to visit in the dark room, saying, "Ethel was a good doctor and he wished her well." Heaven help someone if he wished evil!

Ten years passed. The general practitioners demanded the return of geriatric medicine and were successful.

Chapter 20
Therapies

Mischa's accurate assessment of her emotional need for therapy led her to Eileen Klein, a childhood friend and transactional analyst, author of *Discover Your Real Self* and *How to Choose a Mate.*

Having previously explained that her chances of getting along with Martin for more than two days were nil because he was "B strong" and she was a "Please" character, she chose her.

Eileen was very much into Taibi Kahler's classification of the five main personality types: "Please Me," "Be Strong," "Hurry Up," "Be Perfect," and "Try Hard." Only children tend to be "Please Me" types, as they have to please their parents. Also known as "The Doormat," they seek to reaffirm a decision like, "I'm misunderstood" or "Nobody lets me be myself." At the same time as staying "nice," they are bursting out with resentful hostility. They see relationships in terms of control and use phrases such as "Really, Ye know" and have horizontal lines on the forehead.

"Be Perfect," the perfectionist (obsessional), is seeking to reaffirm a decision ("I am not good enough") and has had religion in their upbringing. This makes them moralistic and dominated by the parent ego state. They can feel guilty and often double check that the gas is switched off. She fears some terrible consequences if she falls short of perfection. Uses words such as "should" and "shouldn't." Body language: purses bottom lip between forefinger and thumb before speaking.

"Hurry Ups" are those who have lost a parent through death or divorce before age of eighteen and come from a family where there is a lot of tension in the air. The Hurrier is seeking to reaffirm the decision that "I don't belong." Such families screech and rush around, which is frighteningly unpredictable to a child. Nobody has time to give the child many loving strokes. They get him out of the way, if rich, to boarding school. He is accident prone and sees life as futile, so is self-destructive. The Hurrier needs to appreciate that love is not a matter of "all or nothing" but something in between. Vertical lines between the eyes are a characteristic.

"Be Strong," the stoical "stiff upper lipper," gives love in hope of being appreciated, but proves in the end that he is unlovable. He seeks to reaffirm a decision—"I am not worthy of love." He gets bored easily, a brave type who leads his men into battle. A British upbringing as in "being seen and not heard." He classically cracks the joints of his fingers.

"Try Hards" are those whose failed parents subconsciously wish their children to fail also. They fail to "satisfy" their parents and so seek to reaffirm the decision that "I am a failure." They give up quickly but need to see setbacks as inevitable. "I am trying," she will claim with a puzzled look. Only by giving herself permission to see setbacks as inevitable will she be able to achieve success. "I am trying to lose weight," commonly heard, really implies failure. As

Eileen said, "If a surgeon told you he would *try* to take out your appendix, would you let him?" The word "try" suggests failure.

Most people have two of these traits. Ethel is "Please, Hurry Up" (sorry sinner). Martin was "Be Strong, Be Perfect" (cold intellectual). Together they were an incompatible mix.

Eric Berne was the initiator of transactional analysis in his books, *I'm OK, You're OK* and *What Do You Say After You Say Hello?* Transactional analysis involves the three ego states. The first ego state is the parent-thinking one (from parental figures), a function of conscience. The adult state appraises the environment objectively and calculates its possibilities. The third ego state is called the child, which each person carries within. He acts as he did between two and five years old. It is not childish but childlike. One needs to understand one's child because it's with us all our life and it's the most valuable part of our personality.

When two people confront each other, there are six ego states involved. These are as idiosyncratic as people are, so it's important to know which ego state is active during a transaction; e.g., a husband's parent ego state to the wife's child ego state.

Games People Play, another of Berne's books, describes subconscious ruses, which enable people to achieve secret payoffs. A woman may say in front of strangers, "I have a ladder in my tights," to arouse them in a self-destructive game of "Rapo." These plausible games also occur at work and even between countries.

Taibi Kahler added concepts to transactional theory. He helped NASA choose astronauts more speedily by predicting what they do with stress and assessing compatibility between candidates. He also advised the CIA and befriended Bill Clinton, helping him win the election.

Ethel joined Eileen's group in the Gospel Oak attic flat, to stop herself from blowing up at the children and au pairs, so for a few years she drove over on a Tuesday night for two hours. She grew to be a disciple of hers, diagnosing these types by their characteristics. "Be Strongs" always walk a step ahead, just as Martin did, and often choose work in mathematics or accounting.

They would sit around in a group in the darkish room, whose walls were covered with pictures, done by her now famous artist daughter. Some had stories to tell straight out of Oedipus, having been seduced by their mothers in childhood. Eileen, highly intelligent, with a hooting laugh, uncovered quickly that Ethel had been abandoned twice by her father, aged eighteen months and eleven years old. Her "Hurry Up" behaviour was the result, so that she could say that she was abandoned because of her rejecting behaviour not because of herself. This is common in children from neglected backgrounds, leading to delinquency. Suicide may occur. This explained her bad behaviour when she sensed a man was getting close.

The "Hurrier" rejects offers of intimacy, in order to prove that the attempt to get love is futile.

Eileen revealed the collusion of her mother with her stepfather's unseemly attitude, cruel teasing, and put-downs. Also, the mother's conditional love and control, depending on her being "a good girl," is a classic for only children.

Eileen helped with problems bringing up her girls, such as Eleanor suddenly refusing to eat meat. Eileen said, "Allow her two she wouldn't eat." It worked; she chose lamb and beef.

Eileen explained that Ethel had a green monkey, sitting on her shoulder, who grasped within thirty seconds of her meeting a guy if that guy could repeat the trauma of her background. Bingo! Instantly attractive. Whereas a person's green monkey from a stable, happy upbringing would latch onto a guy who could duplicate that successful calm relationship.

The result of therapy was an understanding of why she was the way she was but lacked a cure.

Her outbursts of anger abated with learning how "Please Mes" fill up with resentments like a balloon, then "blow up." Expressing their vexations at the time instead of harbouring them was helpful.

Two years with another therapist, Alex in Queensway, were fruitless. His aim was to cultivate her charm.

Fifteen years later, after a major traumatic event, Penelope referred her to her own strange healer therapist in Norwood Junction, a woman named Sam Broche.

Sam was blond, massive, and faintly suspect living in an old house with her youngish, thin husband. Her room was full of weird statues, candles, and burning incense. Large, furry cats roamed.

A Hindu chakra healer, she put Ethel facedown on a mat while she "unblocked" some of the seven energy centres (chakras) on the spine with her admittedly warm hands. This unblocking and realigning help cure emotional instability, insecurity, and loneliness. Blockage of the heart chakra leads people to put others first, to their own detriment, as it is the bridge between the upper and lower chakras.

After, they spent an hour talking. She was frighteningly perceptive. When she described a new man friend, she turned her head away, thought, then said, “He hasn’t finished with a relationship.”

A later dawn raid established a wife sitting in the nest.

She never knew if Sam was a complete charlatan, but she seemed more likeable to others after these thrice-weekly sessions, which lasted eighteen months. Always eager to grasp the cash before she left, Sam did get her through a bad time.

None of these therapies were therapeutic. As a Noel Coward character remarked, “Therapy only reveals that you were in love with your Rocking Horse.” It cannot make that leap to cure.

On a hike in Israel, she got talking to a guy, telling him about the appalling treatment she had seemed to incite from men and the uselessness of therapy. He promptly and fervently recommended Yael to her; as he was a psychologist himself, she took his advice. Yael was a psychologist at the renowned Herzliya School of Psychology and specialised in EMDR.

Eye Movement Desensitization and Reprocessing was a chance discovery in UK and developed in the US. It has been enthusiastically taken over in Israel for victims of terrorism and war. It is now recognized by NICE, the National Institute for Clinical Excellence, and WHO, the World Health Organization. Prince Harry has just announced that he benefited from it.

How it works is not really known; some assume it causes changes in the reticular part the brain. Others say it dampens the power of emotionally charged memories of past traumatic events, when your attention is diverted.

Rapid eye movements occur just before waking when we are dreaming. Therapy consists of analysis by a trained operator to dig out the basic problem. She then applies a protocol, culminating in a statement, reversing the deeply held conviction. At the same time, the therapist directs the gaze from side to side with her forefinger. This actually works in many cases of post-traumatic stress syndrome.

She drove the thirty kilometres to Holon from Netanya, feeling very low after years of not seeing her daughter and her beloved grandchildren, not really expecting much. Yael was a small, modest Israeli woman, living in a small apartment, neat and tidy. Quietly, over many weeks, she took her back to her early childhood with her mother in Southport and established early hurts and misconceptions she had been unaware of.

When she was ready, she put her through the EMDR. Yael was intent on making her realize she was loved at that early stage, concentrating on her grandmother, after noting a lack in her mother.

Ethel was in a desolate stage. It took time but seemed to have helped, now in cordial relations with family superficially. Who knows what goes on underneath?

She remembers her mother saying, "She will commit suicide if Grandma (her mother) comes to visit," and she used to storm out of the house saying, "I'm going to commit suicide." Ethel didn't know as a child whether she would come back or not.

Since then, apart from odd calls to Yael updating her, no therapy. It is a mixed bag with benefits, relapses, and ambiguities. As Robert Louis Stevenson said, "To travel hopefully is a better thing than to arrive." She may have "arrived" as she is calmer now and things are good with her family. As geriatricians say, "Where there is a will there is a family."

Chapter 21
Back to Israel 1993–1997

Eleanor and Penelope were now students, Eleanor in London, Penelope at Hull University. Ethel consulted Eileen on the advisability of leaving them to try living in Israel again. The therapist felt it was an ideal time and would be good for them.

In the middle of the night, the plan had come to her to leave Ealing and return to the flat in Highgate as a base, now empty. Her mum and Rex had bought a larger apartment two floors up overlooking the golf course. Rex had suffered from chronic lymphatic leukaemia for the past twelve years and moved from Manchester to have her mother nearby. It was not an active disease and could go on for many more years, the patient usually dying from something else.

She rented out the house in Ealing and used the money to support the girls, together with Highgate expenses. The empty flat needed refurbishing, so she enjoyed shopping for new curtains and lights with her mum.

Even at age of fifty-four, she didn't want to spend too much time near Rex, another reason to go to Israel; she easily obtained a post in the Geriatric Department of a hospital near Netanya. Bureaucracy was worse than last time, but she managed to get some immigrant rights with the help of her Israeli cousin.

Bravely or foolishly, she settled into Sderot Chen apartment, which was hers now, thanks to Mischa's advice to persuade the parents to sign it over. He had sent a bouquet of flowers, so happy when he heard that news. She started work on the wards. Newfound friends helped a lot with teething problems, especially Carmen, who seemed to know what to do whenever anything went wrong, such as cockroaches. Ethel put in a solar heating panel on the roof; this impressed Rex on his next visit. Her old friends and loving relatives were in Jerusalem, her former hometown, sixty kilometres away.

The ethos in the hospital was unique. Apart from the benign medical director, there was a parallel "black" force indirectly ruled by the great and aged rabbi who had founded the hospital.

In 1944, the thirty-nine-year-old rabbi, shot in the shoulder, was on a death march to Dachau. As he was losing strength, he vowed, "If I survive, I will build a hospital in the Holy Land." Despite losing a wife and nine children in the death camps, and helping the displaced survivors, he did arrive in Palestine. With donations and hard work, lobbying Ben-Gurion, he slowly built the Hospital and Nursing School, famous for its maternity and ophthalmic department. He also launched the dynamic Chasidic community with its growing seminary.

A black-coated Hasid was placed on each ward, feeding back any religious infraction to the hierarchy. Life was considered so precious that dying peacefully in bed was usually stayed by hauling the patient off to ICU to be intubated and put on a ventilator. Extremely hard for Ethel, who had spent several years attending the Chief Rabbi Lord Jacobovits's house in St John's Wood, to discuss Jewish medical ethics with a group of doctors. They had tussled with modern problems of surrogacy, IVF, and STDs, which he solved by using laws from the Bible such as, "Do not put a stumbling block before the blind," questioning whether to tell a wife that her husband had a sexually transmitted disease. When she brought up the likelihood that homosexuality was somehow formed in utero and therefore inherent, he stipulated that even so, it must be suppressed. He was in favour of surrogate motherhood, warning that one cannot have two mothers. She wondered what he would say about the modern transgender craze amongst very young fourteen-year-olds.

He had instilled in us that one must not prolong life if it meant prolonging suffering. So, when she complained about dragging a terminal patient with widespread metastases to ICU, she was told, "That is England. You are in Israel now." This was an anathema; a good doctor makes death as peaceful, painless, and dignified as possible.

To assuage this struggle, she would walk back from work on the beach enjoying the wild winter gray sea and white-horsed waves.

She joined a synagogue, named after an American hero who had saved many "illegal immigrants" from the British military police.

A good opportunity arose to get known in the community, when the synagogue asked her to give her flat for a Seder Tu BiShvat, the new year for trees and beginning of the ancient tax year. "Seder" means order, and similar to the Passover Seder, a festive meal follows a ceremony around the table. Four cups of wine—white, red, and mixed—are drunk together with tasting eleven fruits, pomegranates, dates, grapes, olives, and dried fruit. The ladies' guild brought tables and chairs; the charismatic Canadian rabbi brought the printouts for the service. It was such a great success that she repeated it herself in London. A novelty copied from the Sephardi Jews.

Her first and only experience of being head-hunted happened a year into the job. She was phoned by Professor V, who offered her a post in Share Zedek Hospital, Jerusalem. Rotem, her guru said, "Why not? You may meet a nice fella there." Where would she live? Problem solved by keeping Auntie Gilda company during the week and driving back to Netanya for the weekend.

Israel was in the middle of the Oslo Accords, signed in 1995 on the White House lawn to the famous photo shoot handshake of Yitzhak Rabin and Yasser Arafat, a beaming Clinton standing behind. Heralded as the end of Israeli-Palestinian conflict, it polarized the people with angry crowd scenes, hustled by mounted police. She was there; it was frightening.

Actually, Oslo was meant to be an interim agreement as a prelude to a difficult final agreement. Israel hoped for security and promised to relinquish control of Gaza and the West Bank. Palestinians expected a halt to expanding settlements. The PLO, Palestinian Liberation Organization, acknowledged Israel's right to exist and relinquish all terror. Israel agreed to recognize PLO as Palestinian people's official representatives.

Her cousin, Rotem, received a recording of Arafat's speech in a mosque in Johannesburg in Arabic, in which he said he had no intention of keeping the agreement. Rotem published it and Rabin said that if Professor T says it, it is true, but did nothing about it. Israel left Jericho with its lucrative casino, and areas around cities and towns in the West bank. However, its fear that the Palestinians would use these territories to launch attacks and terrorist acts became horribly realized.

Israel withdrew their army from Gaza at the orders of Ariel Sharon before an organized agreement could be attained and dismantled the settlements there. A big mistake, with hindsight. There should have been a structured, step-by-step withdrawal. A philanthropic American paid a million dollars to buy the industrial greenhouses growing lettuces, etc. in order to give them to the Palestinians. Days after the turnover, the glasshouses were destroyed in riots of hatred.

The protesting settlers were thrown out of their homes by the military, in scenes hard to watch. Some displaced Israelis are still looking for a home to this day in 2019, forced to live in boarding houses.

On Saturday evening in November 1995, she was watching a huge Oslo Accords support rally in Kings of Israel Square, Tel Aviv, on television. Rabin had sung the "Song of Peace" and was leaving the platform when shots rang out and cameras focussed on Rabin being bundled into a car.

Confusion broke out; a while after, it was announced that Rabin had died in the assassination by Amir, a right-wing Jewish fanatic. The telephone rang. It was Eleanor, who had heard the news at a party in London and knew how upset she would be. Rabin, her hero, for years; the gentle, handsome general from the Yom Kippur war had been killed.

Conspiracy theories abound. Alive, when put in a car, why not the ambulance waiting nearby in case of need? Stories of a second bullet through his back in the car. A bodyguard buried in the middle of the night in a secret ceremony. Like the Kennedy story, they will probably never know the truth.

The funeral on Mount Herzl in Jerusalem was a spectacle for the world. Ethel was able to wander out of the hospital to watch the crowds.

King Hussein of Jordan, in tears, saying he never thought his first visit to Israel would be for this. He had recently made a peace treaty with Rabin. Clinton with his "Shalom chaver (friend)!" Queen Beatrice of the Nederland; Prince Charles and John Major standing side by side; Mubarak, prime minister of Egypt.

What an accolade for this great man. Eighty heads of state in all attended. The nation mourned through song, "To Cry for You." Its simple lyrics by Geffen captured the mood. "The Angels Cried" was her favourite as well as "Tree in a Field." The radio played these melodies constantly, portraying the general loss and emptiness felt by the entire country.

Ten suicide bus bombs were going off around Israel about this time. Early 1996, Monday morning on the number eighteen bus route in Jerusalem, became a horror of weekly suicide attacks. Forty-five people were killed. Children were afraid to go to school by bus.

As King Solomon had said, "This too will pass," and it did, thanks to the security wall and secret services, although Netanya suffered many atrocities in malls and restaurants beforehand. So much for the Oslo Accords.

Share Zedek Hospital was an interesting place. Orthodox but sensible, she enjoyed seeing religious principles in practice; e.g., after a death, a bell rang to warn Cohenim to keep away, as they are not allowed to go near a dead body.

Once, a little boy was very sick on the paediatric unit; all the nurses went on a taanit dibur (speaking fast). They stopped speaking nasty gossip about anyone until the child recovered, which he did. Rising early enough to hear the six o'clock shema (morning prayer) on her car radio and driving towards the Judean hills in the dawn was lovely. but the return journey to Netanya in the rush hour, plus lodging with her aunt, became less of a novelty. She considered buying a flat in Jerusalem. When she told the professor that it would be contingent upon her getting tenure, he assured her this would be so.

An unfinished property in a new area at the top of the hill in Malcha appealed to her. The battle for Malcha, a quaint Arab village nearby, was mentioned in a book by Menachem Begin. She loved the view across the mountains, especially at night with the twinkling lights. Five bedrooms, three bathrooms, three balconies were really too big for her. She started collecting the finances in her head; she would sell the house in Ealing and her stepfather, who was visiting at the time, offered to top up the rest from his deposit account. He had already decided that at eighty-six, he was too old to visit Israel again. They visited his bank in Netanya; she heard him telling the manager that he wanted to give the money to his daughter. Her friend, Itta with the ESP, visited and predicted that she would be very happy there. For once, she was wrong. A puncture on the unmade road may have been an omen.

She bought the flat and went back to London to prepare the lift. All the white goods were bought in a place that specialised for emigration. Heals provided the white leather suite and cherry wood table and chairs, etc. Slowly the lift became full.

On the very day, she watched from the balcony as the lift pulled into the street, Rechov Hadishon, and delivered all its beautiful new stuff. She went back to work to be told by the professor that she was leaving in three weeks. "Why did you tell me it would be okay to buy a flat if you knew I would not get tenure?" He shrugged. Then she knew a Scottish gentleman was not the same as an English gentleman.

She arrived home at Auntie Gilda's, who took one look at her green face and fetched a bottle of vodka. She drank and realised her only way was back to UK.

Chapter 22
Busy Years

Coming back from Israel was not the failure it seemed at the time. She was able to see her grandchildren "in" and her parents "out" over the following years.

The professor at the Hammersmith agreed to take her back on an honorary basis, that is no pay, just for the privilege. She was happy to have the week structured; Wednesday, the grand round, Thursday outpatients.

Returning to Highgate with her mother and stepfather living above her was not optimum. He certainly did not welcome her as he did his guests with open arms.

The girls, now in their early twenties, had both graduated and were working and courting their husbands to be. Eleanor, at a city law firm, had found her guy in law school. This Ethel had predicted in Israel, when she took her clothes shopping saying, "With a ratio of one to eleven Jewish boys in the class, it's a good time to find a husband."

One winter's day in December, she was called up to see her stepfather, who wasn't his normal self. She didn't take as much care as she should, being in a hurry to drive to Nottingham and also hassled from wedding plans.

She disappeared up the M1 to join the Limmud conference, an annual jamboree of culture. Two days later, the admin summoned her to the office and told her that her mother had rung to say Rex was in hospital. She drove home in the winter gloom to find her mum in her pink nightie, bed jacket, and pink bedroom calmly reading a magazine. Under instruction from her doctor brother, her Uncle Robert, she had called an ambulance to dispose of her semi-conscious husband, after he was doubly incontinent in his bedroom. Ethel followed to the Whittington hospital, where he was in a casualty bed, pretty ill, stuporous. It was complex. He'd had a fall and injured his sacrum, was in pain. He was anaemic from his twenty-year-old chronic lymphatic leukaemia and he had a urinary tract infection.

Days on different wards led to Ethel's intervention with the house woman, when an overload of intravenous fluid led to congestive cardiac failure. Weeks later, he was dumped in St Anne's Tottenham, unconscious with rasping breathing painful to hear, sitting nearby. She persuaded his consultant, a colleague, to transfer him to North Middlesex to give him a blood transfusion. All this time she was ferrying her mum back and forth to visit, who behaved stoically but her guts took the brunt.

Shunted back to St Anne's, depression was his new label, following a psychiatric assessment, but that was his Polish temperament. "The only way to treat a Polish depressive is with a Polish psychiatrist," it is said. He seemed totally normal after his first ECT treatment, complaining, "They would not give me a slice of bread," when they visited him on a bright sunny day, the last time they saw him alive.

After the second ECT treatment, he was unconscious again. She was called in the night, told to come, and drove through the back streets of Wood Green. He had waited for her to breathe his last. The nurse said, “That often happens; they tarry until a loved one appears.” She watched him awhile, so peaceful, then rode home and rang Penelope to give her the news. “Never ring me here again.” She slammed the phone down. Double whammy.

She waited till morning to tell her mum, who insisted they take him to Israel to be buried. El Al arranged everything. In two days, they were in Netanya together with Eleanor and Penelope. Three plots in the cemetery were available together, so they took them all, a *smash and grab* as Rex would have said.

They sat shiva in Netanya. She was not sad or relieved, just hollow. She had wildly done everything possible to get him better. It had been unbearable at times, but at eighty-eight, a Holocaust and Russian labour camp survivor as well as Monte Cassino war veteran, he had managed admirably. He had damaged her irrevocably and attempted reparation in money (help with buying property); so, it was intricate, love, fear, hatred, righteous indignation, a farrago.

“Tout passe, tout casse, tout lasse. Helas,” sums it up.

Eleanor’s wedding arrangements were a happy distraction. They arranged the wedding hall in the city, and made a trip to Paris on Eurostar for the wedding dress. After a kosher meal in Le Marais, Ethel threw up outside Galleries Lafayette. Tired on their late return, they couldn’t find the car in the vast underground car park.

The wedding was spectacular. Especially emotional was seeing Eleanor under the chuppa, so beautiful and happy with her young groom. It had its classical hiccups, the caterer falling so short, pizzas had to be brought in for photographer and booming band. Some tables even went hungry, only discovered later. The boisterous dancing and wild atmosphere made up for it. Ethel's speech brought a cheer when she said, "Martin found his niche in my life as the perfect ex-husband." The next morning Eleanor rang her to say, "All that fuss just to have sex."

Penelope, on the other hand, plumped for a Lancashire boy from Rochdale, whose Italian grandparents were patients of her stepfather. They had often conversed in that lingo and even went to the Dante Society together. Ethel was churned up at Penelope's choice of a non-practising Catholic, but she grew to love him.

Their civil nuptials in the Town Hall were combined with a symbolic chupa and breaking of the glass, performed by an American rabbi. Grandma had bought Penelope a beautiful pinkish wedding dress with sparkles; the couple looked happy. Eleanor wore navy blue. Photos in Walpole Park and that was that.

Ethel was thrilled to watch the birth of her first grandchild. She was the earliest to see Gidon enter the world and adored him from the word go. The Pidyon Haben or Redemption of the Firstborn took place a month after the brit. The baby must be bought back from the cohen (priest) in a small ceremony. A lunch in a small restaurant and the infant was draped in jewellery; it was unique.

Penelope delivered Emma to great excitement. Blonde, blue-eyed, she had the same long limbs, favoured by her great-grandmother, mother, and Ethel herself. A dynasty. A synagogue naming on a fine Shabbat in May, followed by lunch in the Highgate flat, with fish rosti on the menu.

Alistair's family joined them. His mother gave her a Magen David, a lovely gesture from a practising Catholic. Emma herself was happy in no time. Ethel stayed overnight at Penelope's to wake Emma up, hugging her and laughing. "You have a baby brother." Joyous times to visit newborn Alan and Penelope and take Emma to lunch after, in the canteen. Eleanor changed after the birth of her second child, Amalia.

Ethel thought of epigenetics, where stress can uncover a latent predisposition as Eleanor became "Be Strong" in Taibi Kaylor's classification for a while. Even her driving changed to hard, abrupt braking. She revealed suppressed anger to her mum. At the time, Ethel surmised, maybe some post-natal depression was behind it. Their relationship continued to deteriorate.

Eleanor had another child, Marga.

Penelope had two more boys, William and Zac, born 2009 and 2011; Ethel adored her grandchildren, still does. It is an open and fresh tie, heartbreakingly beautiful and unsullied.

During this early period, she had the brush with Frederico, also described in the following piece.

Telling a relative, Suzette, of the problem over coffee in Orli, a café, in Hendon was ground-breaking. Suzette was of Moroccan origin and "spiritual." She listened, then said, "Give me a mezuzah from your home and I will show it to my nephew." The nephew had shown mystical powers after an operation for a brain tumour. Suzette took the mezuzah to Israel and handed it to him. After studying the unrolled parchment, he announced, "This woman has had a very sad life; she needs to move from her home."

"How do you know?" asked Suzette.

"The word 'adama'(ground) is flashing," he replied.

Ethel, on hearing this, sent a message back asking, "Could she swap flats with her mother as she lives two floors above?"

The reply, "No, she has to move to another place."

So, she put her name down with house agents and forgot about it. A year on, she irritably contacted them. "Why haven't I heard from you? Don't you take women clients seriously?" Guido, a young guy, answered serenely.

"It just so happens that I have two flats in the area you wanted."

"Let's go." One was in Riverside Court, Art Deco but neglected before its refurbishment. They crossed the main road into a quiet street to a new cabled, low-lying block. The lift took them to the top second floor and they entered this lovely modern, mansard-like hall, skylights high up. The flat was really the loft of the whole block. The kitchen was large in white and turquoise with sloping rooves, two more skylights; in fact, they were everywhere. In wonder, she explored the two bedrooms with bathroom en suite. "Too good for her; how much? An Israeli atmosphere," noting the streamlined air conditioner in a rapid babble of thoughts.

A cousin and Penelope with Zac in her arms came to see it and approved. Guido said after Penelope left, "I need a holiday." She had been so cantankerous.

The finances had to be puzzled out; it was more expensive than the value of the flat, which wasn't even on the market yet.

The swooping diagonal wall in the living room worried her as it dominated the darkish room. She faxed a photo and plan of the flat to a surveyor friend in Israel. A swift response came: "Knock down the wall between the spacious hall and the main room." Brilliant, the builders agreed, and the effect was startling; light flooded the gloomy room from the skylights in the hall and the whole apartment opened into a large, airy space.

She juggled with a bridging loan from the bank. The Israeli builders dropped the price and agreed to her paying in instalments, until she sold her Highgate flat. She managed it. However, it was one of the best things she ever did when she moved to Golders Green. She had loving family and friends around her, great shopping and transport. The isolation of the Highgate flat melted away.

Chapter 23
The Darkest Time

A bounder, Frederico, an Italian Swiss, was the cause.

Introduced by a good friend, they corresponded by email from New York to London. In high expectation, she finally met him in the Netanya flat, but while sitting opposite him on the sofa, a flash of something rotten in his glance hit her; a tall, slim, bald fellow smiling easily and moving sinuously.

This she quickly forgot, accepting him as a successful suitor, a bouquet of white flowers for the Day of Atonement, an invite to his sister's for dinner. He drove her car to Tsippori, to see the smiling Mona Lisa of Galilee, an exquisite mosaic in a Roman villa of an ancient hilltop city. She had noted his dry wallet, prompting her to pay for meals in lavish hotels.

Things flourished between London, Israel, and New York, where he lived. She even flew to Zurich for a weekend, when he was solicitous, lavishing gifts, a raclette divine meal, a concert. He had come to pick up his heavy winter clothes and trunk, which she later discovered to her agony was for a cruise to the Antarctic.

Seeing him off at Ben Gurion Airport in a concrete underground car park, he announced, "I want to spend the rest of my life with you," leaving her thinking she was engaged. She was pretty involved by then. She became suspicious when he emailed from the US that he'd been out to buy flowers for Shabbat. *Who for?* she wondered. He even flew to London expressly to ask at an intimate moment if she would "keep him."

"Yes," she murmured. Ethel must have blanked out a lot because she can't remember now the many doubts about him. However, his elusive behaviour in the US drove her to ask an American friend, who claimed to have worked for the CIA, to help check him out. They sat in front of the screen, excitedly tracing the names on the picturesque sample soaps he had given to her from his workplace in USA. She telephoned one of the numbers on the back of the soap, asking to speak to Frederico.

"Who are you?" she asked. "His fiancée." A long silence.

"They are away in Vermont. I will tell them you called. Give me your number." Thrown by the "they," Sinatra's "Moonlight in Vermont" taunted her with the flamboyant autumnal colours "they" must be enjoying.

Next day, the call came. "This is Joanna," a warm, worried, soft American burr. "Did you say you are his fiancée?"

Then it all came out. He had been living, working, and travelling with Joanna for a few years. Living a double life; she had no idea. They became almost friends, comparing notes. She brought him to the phone.

"You have spoilt everything," he outrageously accused her. They still limped along, her suffering many assorted promises and betrayals until she was ready to accept that Joanna, whom he eventually married, was the winner. ABBA's song lyrics, "The winner takes it all, the loser has to fall," became the signature. His cultivation of a Swiss maiden in this menage a quatre finally put the kibosh on the whole matter.

It is known that two failed romances are enough to cause a full depression. This was number six in her life. A detective's nose had led her in desperate fugues to their "in flagrante delictos." These, she bore doughtily.

However, when Eleanor, Gidon (aged three), baby Amalia, and the nanny came to stay with her in Netanya, she was still under par. She took Eleanor to a spa in the Carmel Forest for a few days. There she noted that she was still depressed, from early morning awakenings, a classical sign, so she joined dawn walks in the forest to track wild boar.

An unhappy period followed. Again, she took a few Mogadon, writing a note in a wildly impulsive reaction to a family snub. Again, she was in Israel. A schism of four years of bleakness ensued, in which there was a complete cut in relations. Bouts of weeping in lectures, synagogue, corner of her bedroom. Years of loneliness.

How did she cope? Boring her friends with tales of woe.

Playing bridge was a lifeline. As Churchill said, "A hobby enables your mind to go off on different railway lines. You return refreshed, with new coping ideas, which your brain worked on under the radar." It helped to forget her excruciating plight, absorbed in the game, which demands complete concentration. She played under supervision; it was grim learning the strict protocol, no talking, no touching the bidding box unless actually drawing out the card. When a partner pulled faces or rolled eyes at her appalling play, her brain would flood with adrenaline, rendering relaxed thought impossible. She graduated to gentle duplicate, so frightening. She could not imagine what the standard one was like.

It took years to play a reasonable game; it's really learning a new language. An ocean. She loved it and persisted; the reward came in a certificate of vice master of the Israeli Bridge Association.

That's when she started going to Sam, three times a week, trekking across London to Norwood Junction. It kept her on an even keel of sorts, she supposed.

After this, anger management with a certificate to say she was cured was provided by Yael in Israel. Yael, whose speciality was EMDR therapy, helped; she encouraged her to keep contact with the children by writing postcards.

Things slowly returned to normal with a bridge of seeing the children chaperoned by Martin on lovely outings to Regent's Park Lake, Gulliver's Fantasy Pleasureland, and Bletchley Park.

We are all growing up.

Chapter 24
A Quick Remarriage and Divorce

She met him through the internet site, J date. Having stated her age as ten years younger, their first date, her birthday, found her confessing her true age. Yoni, a Persian, thirteen years younger than her, slim with black hair and a darker skin, filled the credentials reasonably. A degree from Teheran University, a captain in Iranian army, then smuggled out to the UK thirty-seven years before. He was divorced after a long marriage with three grown sons.

She had to throw him out of the flat, that first evening, at his presumptuous behaviour but he was undeterred. She ignored his frugality, when he asked her to pay for her own ticket at the Festival Hall box office. It was not a wonderful beginning.

Only his lovely aunt and uncle coaxed her, with their delicious Shabbat invitations of choresh, sabze, and green rice with chicken. The warm atmosphere and wonderful anecdotes from uncle, of life under the Shah of Persia, assuaged her lonely sabbaths; she grew used to Yoni.

She kept him at arm's length for months, until he surprised her by bursting into tears of frustration on the sofa.

This cunning move did the trick and the relationship moved forward.

She went off to Israel but refused to see him when he came to visit his sons. Back in Golders Green, they shared concert outings and country walks, which they both loved. His early background had been primitive, she learnt, as he reminisced, of the excitement, the day they came to connect running water to his home in Kerman; before that, they used the well and on Fridays. His father would take the boys to the bathhouse where a man would batter them clean. He hated helping his dad's carpet business in the covered bazaar of Teheran and admitted he "did funny things" as a child, like micturating into the food in the outhouse; this may have been associated with his epilepsy, which he outgrew.

A year later, his aunt suddenly commented, "Why don't you go to the Beth Din and have a quiet wedding?" This sounded agreeable to her single arid life, so on her birthday, Yoni asked her to marry him, sitting opposite, at the kitchen island. They went to see *Mormon*, the Broadway smutty musical, and kept receiving excited WhatsApp messages from nieces and nephews around the world. She asked her three granddaughters to be bridesmaids.

She was not in love.

The small engagement celebration in her flat did not augur well. A relative warned as he left, outside the front door, "Get a prenup!" The next day, a phone call from another. "He's backward, has Parkinson's (he stammers), everyone is shocked; you can't marry him." Upset, she exhorted her sister to swear her true opinion. She claimed she liked him a lot.

The wedding took place in the tiny misnomered Banqueting Suite in Golders Green, just room for six tables of family. The chupa squeezed into a space in front; a cousin played "Bon Siach" as Mia and auntie walked her in. They had to wait for her mother's late arrival, so happy and smiling. The ceremony was kept in England for this very purpose, although she had commented after meeting him to her carer, "That Ethel could do better."

She had paid for a room in Hendon Hall Hotel. She did try, sprinkling petals and hearts on the double bed, but it was not really romantic. She took the bus back the next morning to begin her second bout of married life after a hiatus of thirty-five years.

A reasonable two years followed with trips to Thailand and Hong Kong to buy jewellery for Y's business at the International Fairs. They got on well, going on regular breaks to Kent, Yorkshire Dales, South of France, and Israel to visit his sons' growing family. They enjoyed travelling.

With hindsight, Yoni only grew resentful, when he learnt that her solicitor had prevented her from leaving him the flat in her new will. She had mentioned that casually before the marriage. Generous plans, in case of her demise, had been made, including six years in the flat, at 10K per annum. Fuming at the news, he stormed out to his aunt, who told him, "It is not his problem." He went underground, as his aunt told her; he stopped confiding in her from thence.

One evening, on his late arrival home, she did have a strange feeling that he had been dallying. He denied any wrongdoing. Other clues, such as the abrupt shutting down of his computer when she entered his office, made her ask her son-in-law how to hack it, in vain.

Weirdly, whilst washing up one day, she found herself singing, "I know a dark secluded place, a place where no one knows your face, it's called Hernando's Hideaway, Oley."

Wow, what made her sing that? She always sang that song in the past before catching a male betrayal. Sam had noticed her prescient instincts.

She ignored these warnings, probably in denial. Even the night before the wedding, on the way to the mikveh, she had fallen flat, face hitting the concrete path, reminding her again of Sam's warning, that similar falls are the spirit attempting to leave the body, a sign that the man in question is wrong for you. "Too late" à la Princess Diana, when the bracelet, meant for Camilla, inscribed "To Gladys from Charles," arrived by mistake the night before the wedding. "The tea towels are already printed." Too late. Other bad falls had occurred in the run-up to the wedding.

Into the third year, the horrible, unexpected, and undeserved bellowing began whilst in Netanya. Similar to Martin, petty things precipitated these outbursts, but they were the tip of his angry and guilty iceberg. She naively taught him affirmations, to encourage self-control and stop the shouting.

A visiting childhood friend commented, "You have married the same man again." She endured this verbal abuse for another year. Her cleaner in London was considering leaving as she couldn't take the tension; Ethel's blood pressure didn't like it either.

February, back in Netanya for a wedding, the screws were turning. A refusal to pay the grocery bills and petrol as agreed in the prenuptial. She paid for everything else. A scene at a Jerusalem petrol station, when he refused to pay up, decided her. She quickly settled the bill, got into the car, and drove away, leaving him standing, to make his own way back to Netanya.

In bed that night, he handed her the two hundred shekel note; he had a huge erection, the first time in months. Men so value being mistreated.

Why is his smartphone in a drawer? she wondered. *I never hide mine.*

She snooped, first time. What a shocking harvest! Messages to and from women. In the taxi coming to Heathrow, “Missing you,” “Missing you too.”

Months, years, of assignations with different names, discussing films, politics.

That familiar loss of betrayal flushed away her fragile marital security. Broken, she turned to her faithful and loving Israeli helper for support. “Will you get divorced?” she asked.

She remained silent at first, digesting her nightly returns to his phone, for more revelations. A recent one, “Great sunshine, new granddaughter, Sadistic wife,” referring to petrol episode, she supposed. Eventually, she came out with it. “I’ve been on this dating site for two years,” he boasted.

“Why?”

“I was looking for love,” he replied blithely.

Now she knew where she was. The hypocrisy of his putting on phylacteries each morning, followed by contacting a gentile dating site, revealed his shallow outlook.

She clung to him a little, while she adjusted to the new situation; he probably misinterpreted her behaviour, but so what.

"A grand tu bshvat seder celebrating spring, for eighteen people, went off well in the flat," Yoni commented. "That was tops."

They returned to London. All trust gone, she'd creep out of bed while he was asleep, to check his phone. She even telephoned two of his women, who opened up when she trotted out, "Women should stick together." One said what a rotten fuck he was.

She wasn't ready to go through another divorce yet, so she decided to stick it out pro tem. The months found her frantically checking; his pockets, whatever. She called a detective agency to have him followed. He was aware of the surveillance, to the extent he cheekily asked the lady detective to have a coffee with him after spotting her tailing him.

As well as porn, she noticed a new crop of names, pointing them out. He brazenly bragged, "Oh they are call girls." Nadir was reached upon finding a video of a naked abdomen sweeping across the screen of Yoni in his pyjamas, a damp patch you know where, taken in a hotel.

She grew steadily away from him, so when he came to the door of their bedroom and announced, "If you don't change your will and give me this flat, I am moving out," she was ready.

"Okay, move out," she replied coldly. A few months before, a similar threat had provoked a stab of fear in her. The bond had now broken.

She drove him to his new room in a sad block on the North Circular Road and heaved a sigh of relief.

But no, he comically returned each morning for his breakfast until the cereal box was finished, then continued using his office.

But no, one night, as she was falling asleep, her bedroom door started opening; it was Yoni. She screamed and couldn't stop screaming. Half her brain must have recognised him, but the other half was terrified. He genuflected, begging her to stop, but she couldn't for a long minute.

"I came for the ventilator," he said. He still had a key.

Shaken, she rang her son-in-law, who offered to come, but a strong cup of tea sufficed to settle her.

On Sunday, with Yoni working in his office, a relative arrived to help her. "Go ask him for the key," he bade her. Nervously, she obeyed.

"No, why should I?" he recoiled.

"Give her the key!" My cousin had come into the room by now.

"What's it got to do with you?"

"She needs the key." Yoni demurred angrily. He snatched the key from Yoni's hand, who proceeded to tear his T-shirt across the shoulder.

Unwise move. Muscular chap against an old weed.

Yoni was pushed to the floor and dragged by his legs out through the front door. What a sight! She was nervous at night for weeks, despite her son-in-law coming to change the locks and affix a chain and peephole.

The divorce was easier than the last one. L had recommended a good lady, divorce solicitor for the civil one. The dayan commented on her visit to the Beth Din, "Why did you wait so long?" At the five-hour ceremony, she feared he'd withhold the get but it went through. She doubted she would marry again but it was nicely tied up.

However, a crazy letter, badly spelt, was delivered to her friends and relatives blaming anyone he could think of for the marriage breakdown; he even sent one to a relative's workplace and to her own bank, as her PA had accused him of catfishing. It was at that point she realised she may have been in danger had she changed the will in his favour. A little push at the underground platform and "Bob's your uncle." Dramatic but possible. He even took copies of this epistle to Israel, presenting himself at her hairdresser et al. "A fear of ending up as her Philippine carer," in the letter, inspired the kids to take a funny photo, in front of a huge jar of sweets named Philippinos. In fact, Ethel was his geriatrician, curing his prostatic hypertrophy with Proscar treatment and getting him onto statins for his raised cholesterol.

So that was her second attempt at a longed-for happy marriage. She supposed she must accept some blame; she did humiliate him at times, his dyspraxic driving especially.

"Enjoy your grandchildren and forget about men," she was adjured. Echoing Mischa's stricture down the years when he instructed her, "Go, bring up your children!" and left her alone in England to do the job.

Contented at a mostly stress-free hedonistic existence, she sails along. She treasured a trip with her grandson to the Atacama Desert in Chile and to Stockholm, with Penelope and children to celebrate her eightieth birthday. Even shopping expeditions with daughters or granddaughters, rare though they are, bring much pleasure.

Somewhere, in the synagogue of her heart, she keeps a "hope lapel" to pin onto someone. "Hope dies slowly in the savage breast," as her mother loved saying.

Chapter 25
Journal in the Time of Covid-19

Netanya, Israel, 31 March 2020

The day before she was due to fly to Manchester, March 12 for her niece's wedding, her daughter phoned. "Don't go to the wedding, it's dangerous!" Surprised, she spent the day agonising. The Covid pandemic was spreading nastily, and vulnerable over-seventies would be quarantined in UK for three months. "We understand if you don't come," said Mia, her sister. It was her daughter's wedding.

Wise advice. Her brother-in-law, James, had been on a ventilator for two weeks now. Father of the bride, he had ignored advice to make it a small affair. Apparently, the father of the groom had threatened him. "No big wedding, no marriage." Her sister also became ill with Covid; Ethel had been due to stay with them. So, her daughter may have saved her life.

She cancelled the flight but booked straight through to London. Another call. "Stay in Israel, it's safer! Why stick in Golders Green when you can be by the sea in Netanya?" More vacillation, then she cancelled.

An illegal animal market in Huan, China was the source, probably due to the unlawful sale of experimental animals from the local laboratory, where they had improvised the novovirus related to the Sars virus of 2004. China also denied the virus's origin and existence at first. Rumours of people closed in their flats with iron bars, to die unaided, seeped out of China. People banging on locked hospital doors, begging to bring their sick in for treatment.

Bibi Netanyahu, prime minister, set up lockdown immediately, having learnt from statistics studies at MIT in his youth of the danger of exponential viral growth. This proved prescient and saved thousands of lives here.

Quarantined alone in the flat, no guests or visiting allowed, she took it all calmly. They were permitted to go out only for food, medicine, the bank, or a hundred-metre walk. They queued outside supermarkets two metres apart, then their temperatures were taken. Schools, shops, cinemas, hairdressers, airports closed. The streets of Netanya were a science fiction movie, empty, silent, the odd masked person walking by at a distance of two metres.

Passover, 9 April

Three weeks now of isolation; she had had Olympic training in being alone. Only child, single except for two three-year bouts of marriage, meant she had managed well with loving calls from family and friends. A daily walk with a friend in a "follow the leader" style on the landscaped cliffs, their palm tree lawns overlooking the breakwater in the sea, something to look forward to. Streamer Netflix gave great films and bingeable series. Bridge online, food shopping, free Hebrew newspaper, good books; she was never bored.

The government had decreed they stay at home for Seder night, the first night of Pesach.

A woman's lib. Seder, the first time in eighty years she could lead it herself. No grandfather, father, or husband to officiate. Actually, she enjoyed preparing the Seder plate of the bitter herbs of lettuce (horseradish in England). Memories of her grandmother crying in the garden, as she grated the stinging vegetable, flooded over her. She had loved her grandma, growing up in her house in Southport during the war and where she spent many holidays. A warm, funny woman with a strong Yorkshire accent; she can remember her saying, "Go to Halifax!" in scorn sometimes. She had driven a pony and trap to deliver groceries from her father's shop in Sheffield and seen Queen Victoria. Ethel had spent many holidays in her grandma's house. They shared Doris Day films, buying chips in newspaper on the way home, to the ignorance of Grandpa, waiting. "Don't tell Grandad!"

It was quite an operation, this Seder plate. The charoset, which represents the mortar the Jewish slaves used for building in Egypt, is grated apple, nuts, and wine. A shank bone roasted, a hard-boiled egg, and salt water to represent the tears were all placed in little cups around a beautifully decorated plate. She felt a huge sense of achievement, as she placed it on the white tablecloth set just for her.

She read through the Haggadah, telling the story of the exodus, dipping her finger to spill a few drops of wine to recall the ten plagues. Drank the ritual four cups of wine, by now feeling dizzy and delightful. The first state of drunkenness: she sang the old songs, reminiscent of so many years of Seders, a lifetime in fact.

After on Zoom, she watched the London family partake of their Seder too. Heartwarming to be part of it.

Shabbat, 18 April

A perfect spring day, leaning out of the window, as quiet as a bird sanctuary, the cooing of doves, circling swallows, the emerald flash of swooping parakeets and pigeons tailing each other in the first courting maneuvres. The song lyrics "What's it all about, Alfie?" lingered in her head.

She had just read Shemini, the portion of the week from Leviticus, containing the animals and birds they are forbidden to eat. Lovely Hebrew words like duchipat (hoopoe), chasida (stork), atalef (bat), and many others, a wonder to read and only written three thousand years ago. Flying with a twig in his beak to complete the nest on top of the air conditioner of the opposite flat; arcing in twos, together sweeping away over the roofs in perpetual mating ritual, the birds fascinated.

Yom Haatzmaut, Independence Day, 29 April

Israel was seventy-two years old on this day. Ethel was eight on that great day. No fly past as celebrations were cancelled; only the newspapers and radio celebrated another milestone in Israel's thwarted history.

2 May

Funny how old friends reappeared and made much appreciated contact.

Some world leaders disgraced themselves, President Trump hailing the pandemic a hoax, then telling people to inject bleach, and refusing to wear a mask.

Boris Johnson likewise took a two-week holiday in Chevening and was AWOL for five Cobra meetings at the beginning of the crisis. He ended up ill in a hospital ICU after shaking hands, mask-less, on an NHS visit. These leaders brought disaster to their countries by delaying lockdown and tracking with testing procedures, leading to ghastly death rates. Israel only had three hundred deaths in toto, thanks to Netanyahu's circumspect approach. Iran, where they told the people, "Good Muslims don't get corona," had a huge mortality.

The strict lockdown was working here. The numbers of new cases were coming down, they were relieved to hear.

However, days were shadowed by worry about James, her brother-in-law, still on a ventilator after seven weeks, now tracheostomised. Daily briefings hinted how gravely ill he was, and only the phenomenal medical and nursing care at Crumpsall Hospital was keeping him alive. The consultant was especially talented, having worked in Hong Kong in other epidemics including Ebola. He kept the pressure of the ventilators low, whereas other units ran at twice the level, leading to burst alveoli and explaining some of the high mortality. The medical profession was learning as it went along.

The relief when he came off the respirator was euphoric but tempered when he remained asleep and took time clearing the sedation. He was too weak to move even his fingers at first and had terrible nightmares.

21 May

Spoke to James on this day. He answered the phone, a miracle! Was nearly crying; he found the physio painful. She asked him why and he replied, “I get dizzy, been on my back for three months.” So, he knew, the social workers had said not to tell him at first, it being such a shock. Rip Van Winkle of the twenty-first century.

Benefits of the status quo were interesting. They were all sleeping more; I’d wake after a twelve-hour slumber, looking at the clock in wonder. Eleanor rang regularly maintaining interesting and jolly supportive contact. Three of her friends lost parents from the coronavirus; one lost both parents. Was this a factor in making her appreciate having a live mother?

Penelope did not ring, but she caught glimpses of her smiling on William’s eleventh birthday. Long blonde hair. “You look good,” she murmured.

Peace and quiet, self-indulgence, a steak for one; a whole tin of asparagus; weights up by a kilo. Lots of books, *American Dirt*, *Where the Crawdads Sing*, read on the Kindle in three days, so good.

24 May 2020

Twenty years today, at night, the Israeli army left Lebanon under fire. Barak, the PM, claimed a victory, but it was seen by the Arabs and world as a humiliation for the Israel Defence Force. The Mothers’ Organisation had lobbied hard to save their boys, who were getting slaughtered, a fraught decision, correct but badly executed.

Nasrallah, Hezbollah leader, gloated, saying, “Israel is feebler than a spider’s web.”

If a small number of Hezbollah fighters could lead to the retreat of the Israeli Army, "Why can't we do the same?" thought the Palestinians, initiating the second Intifada.

Israel has been fighting Iran's proxy, Hezbollah, now for forty years. Ayatollah Khamenei, the supreme leader, yesterday flaunted a Nazi picture saying, "We have to complete the Final Solution and wipe the Zionist state off the map."

Under the noses of the IAEA (International Atomic Energy Authority), the Iranians were enriching uranium at a frightening rate; six months to a nuclear warhead. Trump's sanctions were weakening but not conclusively due to Russian, Chinese, and Pakistani help. She devoured the newspapers, using a dictionary, of the Iranian attempt to build a corridor to the Mediterranean via Syria, Iraq, and Lebanon, a goal of Persian empires since antiquity.

She often heard the planes early morning, flying their missions to hinder Iranian forces from bringing advanced munitions into Syria to threaten Israel, part of "Operation Chess." Felt good how the young pilots were protecting us.

Ethel was involved with Israel's history because they grew up together and she could see its poor advocacy in not explaining the Palestinians' refusal three times in history, 1917, 1948, 1997, to take Gaza and the West Bank for a Palestinian state. They wanted all or nothing. The recurrent, yearly veto by the UN to prevent Israel from resettling the Palestinian refugees, in order to keep the camps going as anti-Israeli propaganda. If an Arab refugee accepted rehousing by Israel, outside the camp, he was murdered as a collaborator by his fellow Palestinians. An upsetting sore, especially when the BBC has endorsed this ignorance.

The army was preparing for the next war by improving the poor communications between pilots and other units, lessons from the failures of the second Lebanon War in 2006. Technology, advanced algorithms, precision weapons, and anti-drone laser weapons all contribute to multidimensionality plans to reduce casualties. No more piecemeal wars.

6 June

"No flights anywhere," she said to herself. "I'm getting a bit weary and miss my family. It has been eight months." Israel was beginning its second wave of Covid after opening up schools and commerce.

Ethel felt that Netanya was her second home; she would breathe a sigh of pleasure on her first morning back. The fragrant cream frangipani, the crimson hibiscus hedges, pale blue plumbago, and air of mild relaxation under blue skies.

It had such a village atmosphere initially; she loved bumping into friends in the streets, seeing familiar faces everywhere in the newsagent, chemist, and bakery. Still does. Thanks to the dynamic female mayor, Miriam Feyerberg, the centre had been transformed from a slightly vulgar place looked down upon by Israelis, as it was infested with Russian and home-grown Mafia. They extorted protection money, firing shops; shootings were not unknown.

One night after a party in her flat, she awoke to the sounds of fire engines and ambulances. She looked out the window to see a flaming car in the corner. It had been fired in their own backyard. Miriam (everyone is called by their first name) used "development money" from the government to pedestrianise and glamorise dramatically the grubby square. There were shoot-up fountains, where children played, jumping up and down to cool themselves off. Now a university town, with a whole new young area of cheaper apartments, nestled between beautifully, landscaped gardens and multicoloured, street artworks of sports and animals, which raised morale as one went about one's way.

People were complacent; one in ten wore masks, mostly the elderly. The beaches were packed. No distancing here or in UK. Curious, she stopped an orthodox man on a walk. "Why aren't you wearing a mask?"

He replied, "Was your father a Kapo?" Flabbergasted, she murmured, "I am a doctor." He walked on talking to his wife.

Why the Haredim (extreme orthodox) flagrantly breaking all Covid safety rules worldwide is the question. Multiple children in tiny, cramped apartments, as well as absence of radio, TV, and newspapers, meant they lived in a parochial bubble. No excuse for these "murderers."

Live TV was horrifying her. George Floyd, a black man in Minneapolis, allegedly served a forged twenty-dollar bill; he was kneed in the neck for nine minutes by a police officer and whimpered, "I can't breathe." He died, surrounded by shocked watchers screaming, "Stop!" Neck asphyxiation is usual in some police forces. President Trump ordered in the National Guard to stop the violent protests and looting all over the state, the worst in American history.

Her life was opening up a little, invited out for meals on Shabbat. Zoomed family today all smiles, comforting.

She was proud of the seven countries with astonishing statistics led by women. Tsashe Ing-Wen of Taiwan introduced hundreds of measures in January at first sign of the new disease; six deaths. New Zealand's Jacinda Arden immediately closed borders. Iceland, Finland, Norway, all single-figure mortality.

1 July

Booked plane to London BA, 22 July. Still dangerous there, hundreds a day dying, crowds on the beach, huge maskless queues down Oxford Street when Primark reopened.

22 July

Flight cancelled twice.

Frightening cyber battles with Iran. They tried to poison the water supply, zapped just in time by Mossad. We attacked their port facilities. "Someone" attacked the advanced centrifuge factory in Natanz, Iran, followed by other mysterious explosions around the country. Possible culprits: the Cheetahs, an internal antagonistic group together with US and Israel.

9 September

Back in London three weeks now.

Old Yiddish saying, "The shorter the meeting, the greater the simcha (happiness)." Lovely. So good to see the family again, albeit in a flash as they were off on holiday.

Civil disobedience, why? People gathered in large raves, weddings, wearing no mask. Research claims these masksless folks tend to be psychopathic and lack empathy.

The world was waiting anxiously for a vaccine. Not China. "Not a single case now," they said.

Long Covid is a syndrome of fatigue, muscle weakness of hands and arms continuing for months. More serious complications are heart and central nervous system disease. Work in progress.

Her life was pretty much the same as in Israel; she had seen Penelope and the children once; they came for supper. Grown inches and gorgeous.

16 October, Eighty-First Birthday

Lunch with Eleanor at Coal Office in Granary Square, a spacious new plaza opposite King's Place.

Warm birthday tea at Penelope's, a sumptuous chocolate raspberry cake and candles. Felt very blessed with beautiful grandchildren around the table.

Seventeen thousand new cases yesterday in the UK. Boris Johnson was stumped as to what to do, torn between economic hardships and lockdown advice. Ethel didn't feel sorry for him; his feckless attitude until now reaped the whirlwind.

Awareness of cytokine storm, an overreaction of immune system in very sick patients, was giving rise to new therapies.

11 November

She awoke, feeling sad today, remembering the shocking news of Lord Rabbi Jonathan Sacks, their brilliant spokesman's demise. The fates are on the move; Trump lost the election. She put the Malcha flat on the market today.

18 December

Celebrated with Israel the peace made with four countries, UAR, Bahrain, Sudan, and Morocco. Dubai was full of Israeli tourists and fruit in their markets, all thanks to Donald Trump.

1 January 2021

She had the Pfizer vaccine yesterday. The GP rang and told her to go to Edgware medical centre, where they had a hundred vaccines left over. Relieved, she drove quickly to the marquee reception point, was checked, and was hustled in to be given the injection by a sweet lady doctor.

15 January

Saw the first snowdrops today in the beautiful park on East End Road, Finchley, softening the grim news of 1,600 dead daily from the virulent and highly infectious Kent variant, as the spike protein on the virus was changing.

When would it ever end?

Trump impeached for inciting violent crowds to storm the Capitol. Five dead. She had forecast on his election that he would either be assassinated or impeached.

We plodded on with underlying fear that the vaccines might be resistant to these variants.

21 January

President Biden sworn in on this day.

Sad to see Donald go. A video came in Hebrew, thanking him for the four peace treaties. Also, for recognizing the Golan Heights, for moving the American Embassy from Tel

Aviv to Jerusalem, for cancelling nuclear treaty with Iran, and for fighting BDS (boycott, divestment, and sanction).

He was good for US too, lowering unemployment and taxes. He made NATO countries pay their share; China was challenged by Trump.

Apologies for being aficionado of politics; where did it stem from?

Perhaps from the children's newspaper her father ordered, together with a weekly comic. Perhaps from her absorption in the well-being of the State of Israel. Admittedly, a fondness for intrigue and gossip, a way of gleaning information. Behind the headlines, The *Times* would reveal a fascinating tangle in 10 Downing Street recently, when misogynistic Dominic Cummings was pushed out by the fiancée of the prime minister. So much was going on within those walls.

One can read in the daily paper a bigger picture of epic power games between countries; only years later one finds out what really happened, thus touching history.

Her key experience with politics came when as consultant, she was the victim of strategic manoeuvres in the hospital. Lady doctors became the butt of "jokey" female mutilation.

1 February

Vaccination nationalism. France and the EU slating the AstraZeneca vaccine.

12 February

Israel reduced the threat of a nuclear bomb, from three months to five years, by a feat of Mossad. Fakhri Zadeh, the "father of everything," was assassinated. The massive Iranian archive of thirty-two giant safes, blasted open in 2018, and smuggled back to Israel, uncovered him. He commanded the making of potential nuclear bombs, fifteen times stronger than Hiroshima.

After eight months of tailing him intimately, the team of twenty agents killed him, by using a one-ton remote-controlled gun, smuggled in pieces onto a pickup truck parked by the side of the road.

It was done to stop the new President Biden from entering another flawed nuclear deal as he had promised.

23 February

"The end is in sight." Headline in *The Times* on this day. Boris Johnson unveiled one-way road out of the lockdown in stages up to June. Seventeen million had been vaccinated in UK so far but the pandemic was not over.

Yesterday, ten thousand new cases were reported and four hundred deaths; zero Covid won't happen. It will be like the flu, needing probable new vaccines yearly. Eight million dead worldwide.

She would stop the journal now except if she got Covid herself.

Chapter 26
A Woman of Her Time

She is here aged eighty-one, sitting in her office with its skylights to a clear blue heaven. Peaceful, freed from exams, work with its politics and family heartbreaks. The things she went through came into the national awareness, via the media, at the same time. Her stepfather's emotional and attempted sexual abuse was at first a dark secret. Now one cannot escape. It's in newspapers, plays, and books ad nauseam. And so on, through spousal to the third generational abuse. She was not the only lady doctor arriving at work with bruises.

The moniker "victim" is thrown at her in the family. She tries to understand why. Was it the bombardment of her stepfather, Rex, during her adolescence of "Imbecile, cretin"? His constant cruel teasing and putdowns? Her stepfather was probably suffering from agitated depression, but this does not forgive his sexual harassment. She had to grow up quickly in survival mode and missed out on a phase of childhood. To a victimized girl, it was intimidating. She brought out the bully, especially in men, a connection proven in battered wives, who often suffered so in their childhood.

Simone de Beauvoir would concur in her book, *The Second Sex*, along with Betty Friedan in her *Women's Room*, that just being a woman was enough, thus giving voice to the burgeoning women's lib movement.

Or was the victim mentality born much earlier? Yael, her Israeli therapist, gave her EMDR, based on her perception of feeling unloved, very young. The sentence she gave her, during the REM process of following her finger with her eyes, was, "She was loved very much, by her grandmother." Or was antisemitism a factor? At age four, she was asked by another little girl in the floral gardens in Southport, "Are you Jewish?"

"I don't know, I will ask my mummy," and Ethel ran off to ask her.

"Yes," her mother replied laconically.

At primary school, "Go back to Jerusalem!" may be the origin of the Adlerian inferiority complex she developed, feeling smaller than the next person, despite her height. A doctor friend once commented, "You float around the wards in a cloud of inferiority."

The long phase of single parenthood, combined with the full-time working post of consultant geriatrician and all its attendant problems, were just becoming acknowledged, as so many young women struggle with this gargantuan task. It had its repercussions, of course. Grown children, who harbour their resentments like precious jewels. The classic of the good, absent, spoiling weekend dad, versus the bad, disciplinarian, frazzled mum, juggling with professional, parental, and personal responsibilities. "When the gods want to punish you, they grant you your dearest wish," chortled Oscar Wilde.

There were great times. Taking the girls to good theatre, *Equus*, *Coram Boy*, *Chess*. Holidays in Tenerife, Cornwall, Australia, China, Russia. Lovely Sunday hikes in the country with her group, Derech. Coming home, tired but proud, after a nine-mile, riverside walk to Finchingfield, a beautiful village, mentioned in the Domesday Book. She got hooked on birdwatching, which originated from chaperoning Eleanor at school to a bird sanctuary, and spent many happy Sundays with the Royal Society for Protection of Birds chasing elusive waders.

Another modern predicament she fell into was her vulnerable need for love. This made her prey to prowling male predators. The success of locking up that green monkey into the museum of brutal men she had encountered took time, and is not assured, even at her great age.

More about the museum of horrible men, but not enough to embarrass the readers. A collection of betrayers, just the nature of the polygamous male, or was it her mishandling of these delicate flowers? Or did the carelessness of losing her dad twice, at eighteen months and eleven years, reinforce her sense of abandonment? Job: "What one fears most shall surely come to pass."

Butterfingers with the men in her life, who slipped away like sand in the wind, starting with the first, Tom. Only one other, perfect, lord of the realm, observant Jew, thought she wasn't interested, although she was smitten, who married her doppelganger. They both made long-lasting marriages.

Many she rejected, but those she did latch on to were problematic. The Middle Eastern ones were the worst. Especially the Israelis. Beguiling her into a phantasmagoria of the soft and secure romance she so craved. Sadly, her detection talent soon burst these bubbles in sordid denouements. The green monkey did his work well, sitting on her shoulder, grasping within thirty seconds a candidate who would repeat the childhood pain.

Twice, she was caught up with a double life. One, a wartime Kellarkinde with social personality disorder, stemming from identification problems. Could be a book himself. She colluded, long after, because breaking that bond is hard. Ernest Hemingway said, "The only way to know if you can trust someone is to trust them." So, it has been.

The mixture of the ensuing heartbreaks and premenstrual GABA-induced tension led to bad temper. Women got through it somehow. The children were the casualties.

Ethel is basically a happy person, enjoying the enchanting, variegated greens of nature, its trees and flowers. It's "other" people who make her miserable. She now realizes, "We humans, with the situations they produce, are puzzles, which somehow get solved over time." Martin, her first husband's "callous" behaviour, can possibly be explained by the newly acknowledged Asperger's syndrome. Compassion and forgiveness come with knowledge. Asperger's is now a common reason for marital breakdowns. Martin's bullying behaviour presaged coercive control being made a crime, forty years later.

Newly recognised sexual addiction, similar to drug and gambling habit disorders, explains some of men's profligacy. Due to dopamine, of which we have ten different forms in our brains. The many factors causing aberrant behaviour is a science in itself, criminology.

Paedophilia is another horror, the cause of which is unknown to date. The combination of victimhood and psychopathology is fascinating, how it locks symbiotically, hungrily seeking each other. She tries to explain why she became entangled in these emerging dilemmas.

A bad zeitgeist issue struck in 2007. A denial of grandparents' rights. In May 2018, MPs called for the government to enshrine in law the right to see their grandchildren. A modern epidemic: Ethel was aware of twelve single parents in the same predicament.

That lonely period was highlighted when Theresa May felt forced to appoint a "Minister for Loneliness" to tackle the solitude of nine million people in the UK. An American comedian called it a Victorian euphemism for a gigolo. Joe Cox, an MP gunned down in the Brexit referendum, reported that loneliness is as dangerous as obesity to health, thus forcing May's hand. Half of university students suffer self-neglect and depression as well as first-time mothers. Not just the elderly. Suicides among self-isolating freshers has been too frequent in this Covid era.

Sybil, a single, sad friend, who made her life as a social worker in Israel from the age of twenty-seven, suffered a series of hopeless liaisons. We would help each other out professionally with advice on our own problems. She was so happy to move to a flat near the famous Dizengoff Street and visit the new buzzing port area of Tel Aviv for Friday night candle lighting in her seventies. She died alone and unnoticed in this flat. Weeks later, an acquaintance realized she hadn`t seen her around and reported it. Poor Sybil was found, her face eaten by her beloved cat.

I have not felt the same about these feline monsters since. Her horrific end struck me as divine justice for cutting her devoted poor family out of her will, in order to leave it to an Israeli charity.

When Ethel told Penelope that a new Human Rights Declaration stated, “Not contacting one’s elderly relative, at least once a month, was a criminal offence,” her daughter retorted, “Call the police!”

What was suppressed before in white ink is no longer. To end on an optimistic tone in true Greek tradition, Ethel hopes that her coetaneous life will continue in the latest statistic that one in twenty are making the century. “Grow old along with me!” wrote the poet Robert Browning. “The best is yet to be…”

Yr Amhortreadwy

A Phortreadau Eraill

John Owen
Nadolig '09